THE CIDER HOUSE RULES

Part 2: In Other Parts of the World

ADAPTED BY
PETER PARNELL

FROM THE NOVEL BY
JOHN IRVING

Conceived for the Stage
by **TOM HULCE, JANE JONES**
and **PETER PARNELL**

DRAMATISTS
PLAY SERVICE
INC.

THE CIDER HOUSE RULES
PART TWO: IN OTHER PARTS OF THE WORLD
Copyright © 1996, 1998, 2000, 2001, Peter Parnell

The Novel
Copyright © 1985, Garp Enterprises, Inc.

All Rights Reserved

poses of advertising, publicizing or otherwise exploiting the Play and/or a production thereof. The name of the Adapter must appear on a separate line, in which no other name appears, immediately beneath the title and in size of type equal to 50% of the size of the largest, most prominent letter used for the title of the Play. In addition, the name of the Author of the novel must appear on a separate line, in which no other name appears, immediately beneath the name of the Adapter and in size of type equal to 50% of the size of the largest, most prominent letter used for the title of the Play. In addition, the names of the Conceivers of the stage adaptation must appear on a separate line, in which no other name appears, immediately beneath the name of the Author of the novel and in size of type equal to 50% of the size of the largest, most prominent letter used for the title of the Play. No person, firm or entity may receive credit larger or more prominent than that accorded the Adapter, the Author of the novel and the Conceivers of the stage adaptation. The billing must appear as follows:

THE CIDER HOUSE RULES
PART TWO: IN OTHER PARTS OF THE WORLD
Adapted by Peter Parnell
From the novel by John Irving
Conceived for the Stage by Tom Hulce, Jane Jones, and Peter Parnell

In addition, the following acknowledgment must appear on the title page in all programs distributed in connection with performances of the Play:

"The Cider House Rules, Part Two: In Other Parts of the World"
was originally produced
by the Seattle Repertory Theatre, Seattle, Washington.

SPECIAL NOTE ON SONGS AND RECORDINGS

For performances of copyrighted songs, arrangements or recordings mentioned in this Play, the permission of the copyright owner(s) must be obtained. Other songs, arrangements or recordings may be substituted provided permission from the copyright owner(s) of such songs, arrangements or recordings is obtained; or songs, arrangements or recordings in the public domain may be substituted.

A NOTE ON THE STAGING

THE CIDER HOUSE RULES, Parts One and Two, is meant to be performed on a largely bare set. The medical tools used in the original production — forceps, dilators, gurneys, etc. — were real, but many of the major set elements — any cars, trucks, abandoned buildings, etc. — were created with a set of wooden chairs and an occasional plank.

DR LARCH's dispensary was suggested by a chair, a low bench, and an old typewriter (which also was needed for a plot point in Part Two). Most doors were mimed, but their sound effects were used, as were the effects of birds chirping, hawks flying, logs jamming, cars honking, wind howling, rain falling — often made by the acting company itself.

Ladders and old-fashioned apple-gathering baskets were used to create Ocean View in Part Two. Again, a few chairs side by side suggested the white Cadillac that the Worthingtons own. The set design structure allowed for enough stairs, nooks, and a bridge which served as a road, as the sky from which a company member might drop some snow, and as the cider house roof, among other things.

The narrative in the play is not meant to be treated as conventional narration. Rarely should it be directly addressed to the audience. Most of the time, the narrative line is expressed as action and should be acted to the other characters in the scene as if it were dialogue.

If possible, it's nice to have live musicians weaving through the story. The effect of music, lighting and the actors telling a story to each other are the elements that make the evening sail.

And that orphan dropping little bits of snow from above is also very nice.

THE CIDER HOUSE RULES, PART TWO: IN OTHER PARTS OF THE WORLD was produced by the Mark Taper Forum (Gordon Davidson, Artistic Director; Charles Dillingham, Managing Director; Robert Egan, Producing Director) at the Center Theatre Group/Music Center of Los Angeles County in Los Angeles, California, on June 14, 1998. It was directed by Tom Hulce and Jane Jones; the set design was by John Arnone; the lighting design was by James F. Ingalls; the original music and sound design were by Dan Wheetman; the costume design was by David Zinn; and the stage managers were Mary K. Klinger and Lisa J. Snodgrass. The cast was as follows:

MELONY	Jillian Armenante
FUZZY STONE/MARY AGNES	Tom Beyer
OLIVE/MA PETTIGREW	Janni Brenn
NURSE EDNA/SQUEEZE LOUISE	Jane Carr
DEBRA/NURSE CAROLINE	Rebecca Chace
ABORTION WOMAN/FACTORY WORKER 1	Jeff Daurey
CURLY DAY/MUDDY	Danyon Davis
MUSICIAN 1/THIN WOMAN/FACTORY WORKER 2	Joy Gregory
HOMER WELLS	Josh Hamilton
MR. ROSE	Kevin Jackson
MUSICIAN 2/FOREMAN	Edd Key
PEACHES/ROSE ROSE	Casey Lluberes
RAY/CHARLEY/BOB	Dougald Park
MRS. EAMES/LORNA	Liann Pattison
CANDY	Myra Platt
HERB/WALTER/EDDY	Mike Regan
JACK/MUSICIAN 3	Mark E. Smith
MRS. GROGAN/BIG DOT	Jayne Taini
NURSE ANGELA/DORIS/FLO	Brenda Wehle
ANGEL	Shane West
WALLY/YOUNG LARCH	Patrick Wilson
DR. WILBUR LARCH	Michael Winters

CHARACTERS

ABORTION WOMAN
ANGEL
BIG DOT
BOB
CANDY
CHARLIE
CURLY DAY
DEBRA
DORIS
DR. WILBUR LARCH
EDDY
FACTORY WORKERS
FOREMAN
FLO
FUZZY STONE
HERB
HOMER WELLS
JACK
LORNA
MA PETTIGREW

MARY AGNES
MELONY
MR. ROSE
MRS. EAMES
MRS. GROGAN
MUDDY
MUSICIANS
NURSE ANGELA
NURSE CAROLINE
NURSE EDNA
OLIVE
PEACHES
RAY
ROSE ROSE
SQUEEZE LOUISE
THIN WOMAN
WALLY
WALTER
YOUNG LARCH

PLACE

St. Cloud's, Maine, and other parts of the world.

TIME

192_ to 195_.

Note: The dating of years, such as 192_, should be spoken as 1920-something and is a convention borrowed from the novel.

THE CIDER HOUSE RULES

PART 2

IN OTHER PARTS OF THE WORLD

ACT ONE

The company gathers.

ENTIRE COMPANY. Here in St. Cloud's,

OLIVE. In St. Cloud's, Maine in 192__,

LARCH. Doctor Wilbur Larch, founder of the St. Cloud's hospital and orphanage and the director of the boys' division, was assisted in his duties by

NURSE EDNA. Nurse Edna (who was in love with Doctor Larch),

ENTIRE COMPANY. And

NURSE ANGELA. Nurse Angela (who wasn't),

ENTIRE COMPANY. And by

MRS. GROGAN. Mrs. Grogan, who ran the girls' division.

LARCH. He was an obstetrician. He delivered babies into the world. His colleagues called this

ENTIRE COMPANY. "The Lord's work."

LARCH. And he was an abortionist. He delivered mothers, too. His colleagues called this

ENTIRE COMPANY. "The Devil's work."

SMOKEY. But it was ALL the Lord's work to Wilbur Larch.

LARCH. Everything we do, we do FOR the orphans. We deliver THEM!

EDNA. It was not until 193__, that they encountered their first problem.

HOMER. His name was

ENTIRE COMPANY. Homer Wells.

NURSE ANGELA. Homer Wells came back to St. Cloud's so many times, after so many failed foster families, that he began to think of St. Cloud's as his home.

HOMER. I'd like to stay, Doctor Larch. I'd like — I want to stay.

LARCH. Well, then, Homer, I expect you to be of use.

HOMER. For Homer Wells this was easy. Of use, he felt, was all that an orphan was born to be.

CURLY DAY. One day, walking back from the incinerator, Homer saw something on the ground.

WILBUR WALSH. He ran with it, straight to Doctor Larch.

HOMER. I found something.

LARCH. It was about three months — at the most, four. Not quite quick, but almost.

HOMER. What is it?

LARCH. The Lord's work.

HOMER. The Lord's work?

LARCH. Yes, Homer. The Lord's work.

NURSE ANGELA. And so his education began.

LARCH. I'm going to teach you surgery, my boy. You're going to be my assistant.

MRS. GROGAN. And Melony taught him, too.

MELONY. Lucky pony. Promise me, Sunshine. Promise me. If I stay, you stay.

HOMER. I promise.

NURSE EDNA. But how long would he stay?

NURSE ANGELA. With his discovery that a fetus — as early as eight weeks — has an expression, Homer Wells felt in the presence of what some call a soul.

HOMER. I won't perform an abortion. Not ever.

LARCH. Perhaps you're having second thoughts about becoming a doctor.

HOMER. I never really had a first thought about it. Never said I wanted to be.

CANDY. Hi. I'm Candy Kendall.

HOMER. Homer Wells.

WALLY. I'm Wally Worthington. I've got an idea. Why not come back with us? We can pick up some trees and bring them back here to plant. Apples. An orchard.

HOMER. *(To Larch.)* He's a real Prince of Maine, Doctor Larch! He's a real King of New England!

LARCH. Of course you should go, Homer. It's — a great opportunity.

NURSE EDNA and NURSE ANGELA. You mean HE'S LEAVING?

LARCH. It will just be for two days. Although I've told him he can stay longer — if he likes it there.

NURSE ANGELA. We just have to see that he'll be provided for there. That he'll be kept safe.

LARCH. I'll see to that. *(To Wally.)* It's his heart.

WALLY. His heart?

LARCH. He has a weak one, he told Wally. It wasn't true, of course. It was Wilbur Larch's way of protecting Homer Wells.

WALLY. Gosh.

LARCH. He needs to be kept safe. But he did not tell this to Homer Wells …

CANDY. And so Wally and Candy drove back to Heart's Haven

WALLY. That very same day,

HOMER. And took Homer Wells back with them.

CURLY DAY. Traitor!

MELONY. A promise! A promise broken! I'm going to find you, Sunshine!

CURLY DAY. Traitor!

LARCH. Dear Homer, Please be happy. Please be healthy. Please be careful.

MELONY. I'm going to find you!

HOMER. I've never seen a lobster before.

WALLY. Homer. Buddy. We're going to change all that. It's high time you had some FUN! *(The stage transforms into a picture of life at Heart's Haven.)*

HOMER. Dear Doctor Larch … I'm sorry I haven't written in a few weeks. So many things have been going on! The harvest has begun! Candy and Wally are wonderful. I go everywhere with them. I sleep in Wally's room. I wear his clothes. It's great that

9

we're the same size, although he is stronger. I'm learning the back-stroke in the Worthington's private pool.

CANDY. Keep practicing, Homer. And stay out of the deep end.

HOMER. Mrs. Worthington, Wally's mother, says she thinks

OLIVE. Every boy should know how to drive and swim.

WALLY. *(Tossing car keys.)* Here are the keys to the truck. Back her out of the garage.

HOMER. She says she hopes you feel the same.

LARCH. Here in St. Cloud's, it is imperative to have good obstetrical procedure, and to perform a dilation and curettage. In other parts of the world, they learn how to drive and swim!

HOMER. Six days a week I work with Wally and the new crew boss in the orchards. His name is

MR. ROSE. Mr. Rose. I'm takin' over for the old boss. He's dead tired of travelling.

HOMER. Mr. Rose has been teaching me how to pick.

MR. ROSE. Cup the fruit and twist slightly. Pull gently. If you pull too hard, you'll pull off next year's blossom, and it won't bear any fruit.

HOMER. Too quick?

MR. ROSE. Go slow. You bruise that fruit, what's it gonna be good for?

HOMER. Just cider.

MR. ROSE. That's right. Cider apples is only a nickel a bushel.

HOMER. Okay.

MR. ROSE. Sure. Everything's gonna be okay. You come to the first press. I'm sure you got better things to do — watch movies and stuff — but you come and watch us make some cider.

OLIVE. Dear Doctor Larch, Enclosed, please find a check, and consider it a donation of mine to your orphanage. I am writing to say how happy I am that my son was so taken by the good work being done at St. Cloud's that he saw fit to bring one of your boys home with him. I know that Homer was supposed to spend only a few days here, but he has turned out to be a big help to us. It is already clear to me that he has profited from a rigorous education, as he has been learning the apple business as if he were used to more demanding studies ...

LARCH. I'll say, demanding! He's used to near-perfect obstetrics!

OLIVE. I would also like to request that Homer be allowed to stay with us through the rest of the harvest this autumn.

LARCH. The rest of the harvest! Good God!

OLIVE. I am pleased to contribute what little I can to the well-being of the orphans of St. Cloud's. The kids tell me you are doing great things there.

HOMER. On Sundays, I pull lobster pots with Candy's father Ray, who also works for Wally's family. He takes me out on his lobster boat.

LARCH. Do you wear a life jacket on the boat?

HOMER. I find lobsters slightly terrifying. The first thing I thought the first time I saw one wasn't how does it eat, or how does it multiply, but why does it live at all?

RAY. There's got to be something that picks up what's lying around. The seagull cleans up the shore, the lobster cleans up the bottom. They take what's left over.

HOMER. They take the orphans' share.

RAY. That's right, boy.

HOMER. Ray is also teaching me

RAY. How an engine works.

LARCH. You think an engine is so special? I could teach you how the HEART works! Which reminds me … *(Writes.)* Dear Mrs. Worthington, Many thanks for your recent donation. I am glad that Homer Wells has been representing his upbringing at St. Cloud's in so positive a manner. I would expect no less of the boy. I am happy there has been such healthy summer employment for him. Of course he can stay for the rest of the harvest. It should help increase his responsibility for when he returns here — RIGHT AFTER. There is one thing, however, which I must tell you about Homer. There is a problem with his heart …

OLIVE. His heart?! *(Larch swiftly moves to Nurse Edna and talks to her while performing an abortion.)*

NURSE EDNA. He's been learning how an engine works, Wilbur. That certainly sounds different.

LARCH. It sounds silly to me! Curette.

NURSE EDNA. You're going to be fine, dear.

LARCH. No, I'm not!

NURSE EDNA. Not you. Her!

LARCH. What does it mean, he's staying through the harvest? When does the harvest end?

NURSE EDNA. I don't know. September, October ...

LARCH. Early November?

NURSE EDNA. Not that long, surely.

LARCH. Oh, who knows?! He'll come back as soon as he can. At least, he'd better!

NURSE EDNA. And remember the mail, Wilbur.

LARCH. The mail? What about the mail?

NURSE EDNA. It hasn't been answered. In weeks.

LARCH. It's because I'm too busy.

NURSE EDNA. It's because you spend all your writing time writing letters to Homer.

LARCH. He has to know what's going on! He has to be kept informed of all alumni information, of hospital events and social activities!

NURSE EDNA. Why does he need to know all that?

LARCH. He shouldn't be off, playing with lobster pots and beehives! I wonder if they know they've got an accomplished obstetrician tending to their apple trees! *(Pause.)* We're finished here. I'd better go check on that delivery. *(As Larch starts out, Nurse Angela enters.)*

NURSE ANGELA. There you are. That baby boy is waiting.

LARCH. What baby boy?

NURSE ANGELA. For the circumcision. I prepared him half an hour ago.

LARCH. Oh, God, I completely forgot about — why didn't you call me sooner?

NURSE ANGELA. Well, aren't we in a lovely mood?

LARCH. You overordered prophylactics, Angela. We're SWIMMING in them! And we're out of red merthiolate ...

NURSE ANGELA. Yes, well, whose fault is THAT?! *(Mrs. Grogan appears.)*

MRS. GROGAN. Doctor Larch, there's a woman waiting for you. The one you refused this morning. She won't leave.

LARCH. Tell her I'm busy. I've got to perform a circumcision! *(The Woman appears.)*

WOMAN. Doctor Larch. Please. I must ask you to reconsider.

LARCH. I'm sorry. I can't.

WOMAN. So that's it. You won't do it.

LARCH. You're too late. You said it's your fourth month. It's clearly your eighth.

WOMAN. The woman, who had come from Boothbay, said her husband would not let her bring the baby into his house. If I bring it home, he'll kill me — and it.

LARCH. I understand, but the risk is simply too great in a late term abortion.

WOMAN. How much do you want? I'll get it somehow.

LARCH. If you can't afford anything, it's free. An abortion is free. A delivery is free.

WOMAN. I can't, I won't, have the baby!

LARCH. If you have nowhere to go, you can stay here. You don't have long to wait.

WOMAN. Just tell me what you want me to do. Do I have to fuck you? *(Pause.)* Okay, I'll fuck you. *(Pause.)*

LARCH. What I want is for you to have this baby and let me find it a home. That's all I want you to do. *(Woman stares at him.)*

WOMAN. You'll be sorry.

LARCH. I AM sorry.

WOMAN. You'll be sorry! *(And she turns and leaves.)*

LARCH. HOW will I be sorry...?

NURSE EDNA. Wilbur...?

LARCH. *(Shouts.)* HOW WILL I BE SORRY?! *(Barking of dogs. Larch exits as Debra's Mom appears.)*

DEBRA'S MOM. DEBRA! Debra PETTIGREW! It's your BEAU! Hi, sweetie pie! So you're the boy who works with Debra at the apple mart ... I've heard all about how nice you are, and what good manners you've got — come on in!

DEBRA. We have to go, Mom! We can't be late.

DEBRA'S MOM. Late for WHAT?! *(Laughter. Cackles. Huge barking of dogs.)*

DEBRA. SHUT UP! *(Homer jumps in the "car," followed by Debra.)*

WALLY. Homer's never been to a drive-in before.

DEBRA. Really? Gosh!

HOMER. Actually, I've never been to a movie before.

13

DEBRA. Really? Double gosh!

HOMER. You — you seem to have a nice house, Debra.

DEBRA. We just named it. "All of Us!"

HOMER. "All of Us!" Yes, the sign. I saw. I like that.

WALLY. *(To Candy.)* Especially the exclamation point.

CANDY. *(To Wally.)* Shhh.

HOMER. In 194_, when Homer Wells went to his first drive-in movie, the hum of the mosquitoes in the night air of Cape Kenneth was far more audible than the sound track. *(Wally takes out a spray and sprays the car and everything around them.)*

CANDY. What's in that, Wally?

WALLY. Insecticide. We spray the apples with 'em.

DEBRA. Oh, great. Now we'll all be poisoned.

WALLY. But mosquito-free!

HOMER. What are those boys doing by that wall over there?

WALLY. They're peeing, Homer, what do you think?

HOMER. And what are those boys sitting on top of the wall doing?

WALLY. They're peeing on top of the boys who are peeing underneath 'em!

HOMER. And people choose to do this — all this — like that boy vomiting against that fender over there — for pleasure?

CANDY. Oh, Homer …

WALLY. Wait'll you see the picture!

BIG DOT. Hey there, Sis!

DEBRA. Oh, no, it's Big Dot!

SQUEEZE LOUISE. Hiya, gang!

DEBRA. And there's Squeeze Louise!

CANDY. And look who's with her … *(Herb Fowler appears.)*

WALLY. What's Herb doing here? Where's his wife?

DEBRA. He must have left her home …

HERB. Hiya, Homer! Guess you're gonna need one of these! *(He flips him a rubber.)*

BIG DOT. Come on, Herb, can't you ever stop with those?

HERB. Long as there's a demand, why shouldn't I supply? *(He puts his arm around Squeeze.)* Ain't that right, Squeeze?

SQUEEZE LOUISE. Stop it, Herb! I told you to keep your hands to yourself. You're a married man!

HERB. I don't see the Missus anywhere about, do you? *(Homer looks at the rubber.)* Don't you know what to use 'em for, Homer?

HOMER. Course I do, Herb. I've just never seen one in a commercial wrapper before. *(Movie sounds. They all face out.)*

WALLY. It's starting! *(Lights go down. Headlights out. Movie sounds continue.)*

ENTIRE COMPANY. A gigantic image filled the sky.

HOMER. It's something's mouth! Something's head! A kind of horse!

WALLY. It was a camel, actually.

HOMER. A horribly deformed horse — a mutant horse! Some ghastly fetus-phase of a horse!

BIG DOT. The camera staggered back farther.

SQUEEZE LOUISE. Mounted near the camel's grotesque hump was a black-skinned man almost entirely concealed in white wrapping.

HOMER. Bandages!

PROJECTIONIST. The ferocious black Arab nomad whacked the lumbering camel with the flat of his frightening curved sword *(He lets out a great Arabian war cry!)*

BIG DOT. And drove the beast into a gallop across endless sand dunes

SQUEEZE LOUISE. Suddenly

ENTIRE COMPANY. MUSIC! WORDS!

HOMER. What was that?

WALLY. Some dumb Bedouin, I think.

HOMER. A Bedouin? It's a kind of horse?

DEBRA. WHAT horse?

HOMER. Er — the animal. *(Candy turns and looks at him.)*

CANDY. That's a camel, Homer.

DEBRA. You thought that was a HORSE?!

WALLY. You've never seen a camel?!

CANDY. *(To Wally.)* Well, where *would* he see a camel, Wally?

WALLY. I dunno. I was just surprised, that's all.

HOMER. I've never seen a Bedouin, either. That was one — on the camel?

WALLY. An Arab Bedouin, I guess.

CANDY. A Bedouin is somebody who has no home, Homer.

15

HOMER. What are those?

CANDY. Those are credits. The Bedouin is leaving.

WALLY. Here come new characters!

ENTIRE COMPANY. Pirates!

FIRST COUPLE MAN. Great ships were blasting each other with cannons;

FIRST COUPLE WOMAN. Swarthy men with uncut hair and baggy pants were doing terrible things to nicer-looking men, who were better dressed.

HOMER. Oh! Look! And there's a woman!

SECOND COUPLE WOMAN. A beautiful blonde woman whom the pirates had kidnapped —

GUYS IN CAR. And with whom they attempted to make merry with drunkenness and song.

SECOND COUPLE MAN. A man who apparently adored the complaining woman pursued her across the ocean,

FIRST COUPLE MAN. Through burning harbor towns and charmless inns of suggested

FIRST COUPLE WOMAN. But never visualized

FIRST COUPLE. Lewdness.

BIG DOT. As the fog rolled in, there was much of the movie that was never visualized,

HOMER. Although Homer remained riveted to the image in the sky. *(Wally and Candy have slumped down in the front seat.)*

CANDY. No, Wally! *(Homer leans over and peers at them, then goes back to looking at the "screen." Debra stares at Homer. He looks back at the movie.)*

HOMER. I think I've missed something. *(Candy sits up and looks at him.)*

DEBRA. I think you've missed me. I think you've forgotten I'm here. *(Debra kisses Homer neatly on the mouth, then sits back and smiles at him.)* Your turn. *(Wally sprays the insecticide over everybody some more. Everybody coughs. Homer chooses this moment to kiss Debra. She resists at first, then kisses him back. She puts her head on his shoulder, a hand on his chest. He puts a hand on her chest, and she pushes it away. The movie music now becomes the music for a ballet of hands and feet and neck and tongue negotiation between Homer and Debra.)*

HOMER. Tentatively, at first, Homer proceeded to discover a yes-no set of rules. *(Debra kisses him and licks his face sweetly.)* He began to feel like a well-treated pet — certainly better treated than most of the Pettigrew dogs. *(Larch, Nurse Angela and Nurse Edna appear.)*

LARCH. Enjoying yourself, Homer?

NURSE EDNA. A *movie?!* What is it?

NURSE ANGELA. Don't forget us, Homer.

LARCH. Don't forget your home.

HOMER. Doctor Larch? Nurse Edna? Angela? I won't! How could I…? *(They disappear.)* Home?

CANDY. WALLY, NO! *(Debra looks at Homer.)*

DEBRA. What's the matter, Homer? Are you crying? There, there … *(Candy sits up. She touches Homer's head.)*

CANDY. It's okay. You can cry. I cry at lots of movies.

WALLY. Hey, buddy. We know this must all be a shock to you. ("His poor heart," thought Wally),

CANDY. (And Candy thought, "You dear boy, please watch out for your *heart.*") *(She puts her cheek next to Homer's cheek, and kisses him near his ear.)* It was a very sudden surprise to her, how much she enjoyed that kiss of friendship;

HOMER. It surprised Homer Wells, too.

WALLY. Hey, buddy. You okay?

HOMER. Fine, yes. Fine … *(Pause.)* It was a feeling that rushed him from nowhere — was that what love was, and how it came to you? *(Music fanfare as movie ends. Company exits. Homer alone.)* A Bedouin. That's what I am. I'm a Bedouin. *(Pause.)* "Dear Doctor Larch … Tonight I realized something, and I don't know what to do about it … " *(Pause.)* Wonder if I should tell him. Maybe not … *(Writes.)* "The folks here at the apple mart are strange. There's a man, Herb Fowler, who hands everybody prophylactics … " *(Scratches this out.)* Don't think I should tell him about Herb, either. *(Writes.)* "I miss you." No. He'll think that'll mean I want to come back … *(Pause.)* "The swimming lessons with Candy are going well. Candy is so beautiful when she swims. Also, when she plays tennis. And she drives her own car — and knows how to use jumper cables! … " *(Stops writing.)* Candy … At night, when I'm in Wally's room, I try not to think about Candy … *(Larch and Nurse Angela are going through the mail.)*

LARCH. He's fallen in love with her. I'm sure of it.

17

NURSE ANGELA. Good for him, Wilbur.

LARCH. Good? What do you mean, good? It's terrible! If he's in love, he'll NEVER want to come back here! And he belongs here. With us. With me!

NURSE ANGELA. You know such a wish is unfair.

LARCH. Is it? *(Out.)* He couldn't tell Angela how Homer had ended the letter ...

HOMER. "I remember when you kissed me. I wasn't really asleep."

LARCH. *(To Homer.)* Yes. I remember that, too. I remember nothing so vivid as kissing you. Why didn't I kiss you more? Why not all the time?

NURSE ANGELA. Oh, dear.

LARCH. What now?

NURSE ANGELA. This. A letter from our board of trustees. They've decided we need a new assistant.

LARCH. What?! When did they decide that?

NURSE ANGELA. Let's see. About two weeks ago. *(Reads.)* "There have been complaints."

LARCH. Complaints! What kind of complaints?

NURSE ANGELA. About the service here.

LARCH. The service! From whom?

NURSE ANGELA. They don't say. "As part of our annual meeting ... something something ... we feel you could all be invigorated by a somewhat younger assistant ... "

LARCH. Oh, my Lord.

NURSE ANGELA. "Please begin interviewing prospective candidates ... or ask us to help ... "

LARCH. Help? You know what that will mean! We have to write them. We have to stop them. Otherwise ...

NURSE ANGELA. Otherwise they might get wind of what ELSE we're doing here.

LARCH. Exactly. Write them, Angela. Immediately.

NURSE ANGELA. What should I tell them?

LARCH. Tell them we're in charge of the situation. Thank them and tell them ... we don't need anyone just yet. Tell them ... we just need a new typewriter.

NURSE ANGELA. A new TYPEWRITER?!

LARCH. Yes. To update the office. I'll take care of the rest. *(Nurse*

Angela leaves.) They want to replace me. They think I'm too old. An assistant. I already HAVE an assistant. Only how the hell do I get the board to hire him? *(Nurse Edna enters.)*

NURSE EDNA. Wilbur, that delivery's ready.

LARCH. A plan, Edna. We need a plan ...

NURSE EDNA. What?

LARCH. A plan! To get back Homer Wells! *(They exit. Lights up on Melony and the company on the road.)*

FOREWOMAN. The next day, in August,

CHARLEY. A hazy sun hung over the coastal road between York Harbor and Ogunquit.

EDDIE. It was a St. Cloud's sunlight, steamy and flat,

MELONY. And Melony was irritated by it and sweating. It had taken her months to search the apple orchards in this limited vicinity. *(To Forewoman.)* You got anything for me to do?

FOREWOMAN. In three weeks — if you know how to pick. We're only pickin' Gravensteins this month.

MELONY. So?

FOREWOMAN. So, I got all the help I need. There ain't that many. *(She starts off.)* I'll give you ten cents a bushel. Only a nickel a bushel for drops, or if you bruise the fruit. You look like you could pick ninety bushels a day. I've had guys here doin' a hundred bushels. That's —

MELONY. Ten bucks a day.

FOREWOMAN. Very good. Come back in three weeks.

MELONY. I'll be somewhere else in three weeks.

FOREWOMAN. Too bad. You look strong! *(Melony walks.)*

MELONY. About a mile away from the apple mart, Melony walked by a part of the orchard where two workers were picking Gravensteins.

EDDIE. One of the men waved to her;

MELONY. Melony started to wave back, but thought better of it. *(Eddie and Charley approach her.)*

EDDIE. You look like you lost your sweetheart. Good thing you found me.

MELONY. You better leave me alone, buster.

CHARLEY. But the other man was already coming closer.

MELONY. She hopped over the road ditch and ran into the

19

orchard.

CHARLEY. The man pursued her, whooping.

EDDIE. The other man joined the chase.

MELONY. She ran down one row between the trees, then up another.

CHARLEY. The first man to chase her was gaining on her.

EDDIE. The other man was big and slow, and he was huffing and puffing after he'd passed five or six trees.

MELONY. Melony was huffing and puffing herself, but she ran with a certain, even strength,

CHARLEY. And although the first, smaller man was gaining on her,

MELONY. She could hear him breathing harder and harder.

EDDIE. Get her, Charley!

CHARLEY. To Charley's surprise,

MELONY. Melony stopped and turned to face him.

CHARLEY. — she moved low to the ground, a kind of animal whine in her throat,

MELONY. Then she ran at Charley, flinging herself upon him. When she felt her knee against his throat, she jounced on him.

CHARLEY. He made a choking sound and rolled on his side.

MELONY. She jumped to her feet and stamped twice on his face,

CHARLEY. And when Charley managed to turn over, on all fours,

MELONY. She jumped up as high as she could and landed with both feet in the small of his back.

CHARLEY. He was already unconscious

MELONY. When she pinned his arm behind him and bit his ear. Feeling her teeth meet, she let him go and caught her breath. Then she spit on him. *(Eddie arrives, stumbling, and looks at them.)*

EDDIE. What'd you do to Charley?

MELONY. Melony rolled Charley on his back and took his belt.

EDDIE. Charley! Get up!

MELONY. Melony started swinging the belt around and around her head.

EDDIE. Hey!

MELONY. Hey, what, buster? *(Pause.)* She cracked the buckle across one of the man's shins.

EDDIE. Where it lifted up a flap of blue jeans and skin that looked like a torn dollar bill.

MELONY. When the man bent over to grab his legs she swiped the belt buckle across his face — *(He sits down and puts his hand to his cheek. Melony smacks the buckle across the bridge of his nose.)*

EDDIE. The force of the blow temporarily blinded him. He tried to cover his head with one arm.

MELONY. But she found it easy to hit him everywhere.

EDDIE. The buckle raked and nicked his spine;

MELONY. Then she strapped him across the backs of his legs and ass.

EDDIE. Good Christ, ain't she ever gonna stop?! *(Melony stops.)*

MELONY. I'm gonna find you, Sunshine ... *(She leaves.)*

EDDIE. Is she gone, Charley?

CHARLEY. I HOPE so ... *(Nurse Edna and Nurse Angela enter carrying a typewriter.)*

NURSE EDNA. Wilbur! Wilbur! *(Larch exits.)*

LARCH. What is it?

NURSE EDNA. Your new typewriter's arrived. From the board of trustees.

NURSE ANGELA. Though Heaven knows what you're going to do with it, now you've got the keys replaced on the old one ...

LARCH. What I'm going to do with it? Oh, I know EXACTLY what I'm going to do with it. Edna, Angela. *(He goes into the dispensary.)* I'll show that damn board of trustees! They want an assistant! I'll give them an assistant! *(Lights down on him. Homer appears. Lights up on the Ocean View cider press party. Music plays. Wally, Candy, Olive, apple mart workers, etc., appear.)*

WALLY. You gonna join us, Homer?

CANDY. You coming to the party?

OLIVE. You can dance with me, Homer, dear ...

DEBRA. And with ME, Homer ...

HOMER. Oh. I don't dance too good, Debra ...

BIG DOT. You get him out on the floor, Sis ...

HOMER. In all of Heart's Haven, nothing reminded Homer of St Cloud's as much as the cider house where the migrants lived, and where Mr. Rose conducted the first cider press.

MR. ROSE. In eight hours of no nonsense, and about three hundred bushels, they had a thousand gallons. *(Migrants cheer.)* Was

21

you bored?

HOMER. No, no. It was very interesting.

MR. ROSE. You got to come at night to get the real feel of it. When you pick all day and press all night, then you get the FEEL of it. *(He hands Homer a cup of cider, solemnly. Homer drinks it. Coughs.)*

HOMER. It's — strong.

MR. ROSE. It got rum in it. *(Everybody laughs and drinks.)* Jack, you're bottlin' now.

JACK. I've been bottlin'.

MR. ROSE. Then you're gettin' real good at it.

JACK. I'll press for awhile.

MR. ROSE. Hero and Wednesday are goin' good. You just get back to bottlin'.

HOMER. So this is where you all live?

MR. ROSE. Yes, Homer. This is crew quarters. Mrs. Worthington always makes it nice for us. She puts fresh flowers everywhere.

HOMER. What are these?

MR. ROSE. Those are the rules.

HOMER. The rules?

MUDDY. The cider house rules.

HOMER. *(Reads.)* One. Please don't operate the grinder or the press if you've been drinking. Two. Please don't smoke in bed or use candles. Three. Please don't go up on the roof if you've been drinking — especially at night ... Four. Please don't take bottles with you when you go up on the roof. What's all this about the roof?

PEACHES. You can see the ocean from the roof.

MR. ROSE. At night, you can see the Ferris wheel and the carnival lights in Cape Kenneth.

MUDDY. We sit up on the roof all night, some nights.

PEACHES. We get drunk up there and fall off, some nights.

MUDDY. One night last year, Peaches got so drunk and sweaty, running the press, that he passed out in the cold storage and woke up with pneumonia.

HOMER. You don't exactly wake up with pneumonia, Muddy. It's more complicated than that.

MUDDY. Really?

MR. ROSE. You can listen to Homer. He's a smart man.

22

MUDDY. Anyway, nobody pays no attention to them rules. Every year, Mrs. Worthington writes them up, and every year, nobody pays no attention.

HOMER. Why is that?

PEACHES. They is pretty dumb, you know? First they say, don't drink on the roof. Then they say, don't take no bottles up there. Don't they know that's the same rule twice?

MR. ROSE. That's exactly how dumb they are. They make their own rules, then they think they're the same rules for us ... Right, Muddy?

MUDDY. That's right.

HOMER. This is the last one. Five. There should be no more than half a dozen people on the roof at one time.

PEACHES. It don't mean nothing, do it, Mr. Rose?

MR. ROSE. Nothing? You think it mean nothing? Who lives here? Who grinds the apples, who presses the cider, who cleans up the mess? Who just plain LIVES here?

PEACHES. I don't know ...

MR. ROSE. Course you do! WE do!

MUDDY. That's right. Then WE make the rules. WE are the ones that make the rules. *(He looks to Mr. Rose.)*

MR. ROSE. *(Quietly.)* That's right. *(Wally appears.)*

WALLY. There you are, Homer. I've been looking for you.

MR. ROSE. Evening, Mr. Worthington.

WALLY. Evening, Mr. Rose. Great first press!

MR. ROSE. Thank you.

WALLY. You comin' back outside, Homer?

HOMER. Sure, Wally. I'll be right there. *(Wally goes off.)*

MR. ROSE. You run along, Homer. But some night ... you got to come see the view from the roof, my friend. *(Jack appears, laughing.)* What's so funny?

JACK. Nothin'. Just. My cigarette.

MR. ROSE. What about it?

JACK. It fell out of my mouth. Into the vat. *(Everybody laughs. Except Mr. Rose.)*

MR. ROSE. Then you better fish it out. Nobody wants that muckin' up the cider. *(Pause.)* Go on. Go fish. *(Jack takes off his boots.)* Not just the boots. Take off ALL your clothes, and then go

23

take a shower. We got work to do.

JACK. I ain't gonna strip and go wash just to go swimmin' in there!

MR. ROSE. You're filthy all over. Be quick about it.

JACK. Hey, YOU can be quick about it. You want that butt out of there, you fish it out yourself. *(Pause.)*

MR. ROSE. What business you in?

JACK. Hey, what?

MR. ROSE. What business you in, man?

MUDDY. Say, you in the apple business, man.

JACK. Say, what?

MUDDY. Just say you in the apple business, man. You know what business Mr. Rose is in, man? He in the knife business, man. You don't wanna go in the knife business with Mistuh Rose.

JACK. Oh, no?

MR. ROSE. No. *(He has moved very close to Jack. He looks him square in the eyes.)* You just stay in the apple business and you'll do fine. Sorry if I offended you. *(Jack nods, backing down.)*

JACK. When he looked, Jack saw that his entire jacket flapped open. His shirt was neatly sliced in half.

ALL. Missing all his buttons. *(Jack gapes at Mr. Rose. Then, he withdraws.)*

HOMER. How … how did you do that?

MR. ROSE. Your hands got to be fast. Your knife got to be sharp. But you DO it with your eyes. *(Pause.)*

HOMER. Like a scalpel.

MR. ROSE. Like a what?

HOMER. A scalpel. It makes no mistakes. Only a hand. Only a hand makes mistakes. *(Mr. Rose smiles and exits. Muddy looks at Homer.)*

MUDDY. Just remember, Homer, about who makes the rules.

HOMER. Right. *(Pause.)* Later that night, Homer and Wally added wood to the bonfire.

WALLY. If I were flying, in the war. IF I joined, and IF I flew, I mean, IF I were in a bomber, I'd rather be in the B-24 than the B-25, I'd rather be STRATEGIC than TACTICAL, bomb things not people. And I wouldn't want to fly a fighter in the war. That's shooting people, too.

BIG DOT. Hey, Louise! You fix your wringer, darlin'? You hear, Homer? Louise's mop wringer was out of joint today …

SQUEEZE LOUISE. It was jammed or somethin'.

BIG DOT. Are you overusin' your poor wringer, Louise? *(Debra laughs. Big Dot roars.)*

SQUEEZE LOUISE. Oh, cut it out!

DEBRA. Louise has got an overworked wringer!

BIG DOT. Louise, you must be stickin' too many mops in your wringer, darlin'. *(They all laugh.)* Too much of ONE mop, that's for sure. Course, that might also be true for others of us out here, huh? Sis? And your little friend over there?

DEBRA. *(Giggles.)* Oh, Dot, now, stop it …

BIG DOT. Say, Homer, why don't you take Louise and me to the movies this weekend? You looked like you were gettin' real experienced at movie-watchin' the other night! *(Big Dot and Squeeze laugh.)*

SQUEEZE LOUISE. Can you remember anything about the picture?

BIG DOT. And Wally — you can take us with YOU, too! *(They roar.)*

WALLY. Feel the chill tonight? Fall's really here. I'm gonna miss you when you have to go home, buddy.

HOMER. Home?

WALLY. After the harvest, I mean. Back. To St. Cloud's.

HOMER. Oh. Right.

WALLY. And Candy's gonna, she TOLD me how much she's gonna miss you, too.

HOMER. She did…? I mean — well, I'm gonna miss her — both of you, too. You have no idea … Wally — I was wondering, but don't tell me, if you don't want to, how it was that you and Candy decided to, you know, not have the baby.

WALLY. Oh. Well. We talked about it. But Candy felt it just wasn't the right time. I mean, that we just weren't ready. For any of it — for marriage, OR for having the baby. You see, we've always planned on getting married.

HOMER. You have?

WALLY. Mmn. But then I got to thinking, if there was a war, I'd want to go, whether we had a baby or not. Only, if there were a

25

child, it wouldn't feel right, going to a war.

HOMER. When would it feel right to go to a war?

WALLY. That's exactly what Candy said. But, I mean, I'd just have to, that's all, if we had one. And Candy, well — she grew up having no mom, you know. She knows how tough it can be, to be raised by only one parent. Anyway ... we finally decided we'd wait on everything for awhile. *(Pause.)* I suppose it seems odd. Waiting.

HOMER. Odd? No, I — not at all. *(Pause.)*

WALLY. Once I'm back at school — and after the harvest, until you leave — you'll look after Candy for me, won't you, Homer? Buddy?

HOMER. Right. *(Pause.)* The rules ...

WALLY. What's that?

HOMER. No. Nothing.

CANDY. Hiya, boys. Care to dance? *(Candy, Homer and Wally dance. Debra joins them as all four dance. They pair off, then switch. Lights down on them and up on St. Cloud's. Larch is in his dispensary taking ether. Mrs. Eames appears.)*

MRS. EAMES. Evening, Wilbur. Tired after your long trip?

LARCH. Yes. Exhausted.

MRS. EAMES. How was Boston?

LARCH. Boston was fine.

MRS. EAMES. What an adventure. To the Harvard Medical School.

LARCH. Yes. To my alma mater.

MRS. EAMES. And the Admissions Office?

LARCH. They showed me what I needed to see. Transcripts. Transcripts of recent graduates. In case one would want to come work here, at St. Cloud's.

MRS. EAMES. And did you add a transcript of your own?

LARCH. Yes. I did. On one of their very own forms ... And now, he and I can start corresponding together ... On his very own typewriter ...

MRS. EAMES. Clever, Wilbur. Very clever. To begin your plan.

LARCH. My plan, yes. *(Fuzzy Stone appears.)*

MRS. EAMES. Fuzzy ...

FUZZY. Fuzzy ...

LARCH. Fuzzy Stone ...

MRS. EAMES. And what happened to poor Fuzzy?

LARCH. He got adopted. By a wonderful family. Name of Eames.

FUZZY. Mommy!

MRS. EAMES. Ah, Wilbur. Always rewriting. Always revising history.

LARCH. Fuzzy Stone. I have plans for you, Fuzzy. *(He goes to the two typewriters. Larch sits in the dispensary, two typewriters facing him. He puts a piece of paper in the new one. He types.)* To Doctor Wilbur Larch, St. Cloud's Orphanage, St. Cloud's, Maine.

FUZZY. Dear Doctor Larch, This is the first letter I'm writing to you since my graduation from Harvard Medical School. Sorry I haven't responded sooner. I've been so terribly busy. In response to your inquiry: I doubt that I will EVER come to feel as you do, regarding abortion. Certainly, it is obstetrics that interest me, and certainly your example is responsible for my interest, but I expect we shall never agree about abortion. Although I know you perform abortions out of the most genuine beliefs and out of the best intentions, you must permit me to honor my beliefs accordingly ...

LARCH and FUZZY. ... The fact is, Doctor Larch, I believe there is a soul, and that it exists from the moment of conception ...

FUZZY. However, I'd love to talk with you further about this. Boston is so lovely this time of year, etc., etc. *(Larch jumps to the old typewriter, puts a piece of paper in, and types.)*

LARCH. Dear (Now) Doctor Stone, Congratulations on your recent graduation from my own alma mater. I must admit, though proud of your already considerable achievements, I am worried by your condescension towards me. Do you think you can patronize me? I sense in your tone that unmistakable self-righteousness which I suspect all supporters of the existing laws against abortion would feel at home with ... *(He goes back to the new typewriter and puts in a new piece of paper. During the following, Fuzzy begins to tap dance as Larch types.)*

FUZZY. Condescension? Not at all, dear doctor. I have nothing but the highest respect for you and your office. In fact, now that I am casting about for common practice, I was even thinking of proposing our working together, in the hopes of replacing — I should say, following in — your footsteps, but not until you're ready to retire, of course!

LARCH. *(Gleefully.)* Of course!

FUZZY. In this way, abortions would not be performed, and a safe and informative view of family planning could achieve the desired affect in St. Cloud's — a minimum of unwanted children brought forth into the world — and without breaking the laws of God or man!

LARCH. He sounds like a missionary — good idea! You sound like a missionary!

FUZZY. I FEEL like a missionary!

LARCH. I will never allow myself to be replaced by some reactionary religious moron who cares more for the misgivings suffered in his own frail soul than for the actual suffering of countless unwanted and mistreated children.

FUZZY. Oh, now, really! *(Larch stands facing him.)*

LARCH. I am SORRY you're a doctor! You are not the proper successor to this orphanage! Over my dead body will you ever get my job! *(Pause. Larch sits back in his chair, exhausted.)*

FUZZY. *(Curtly.)* Dear Doctor Larch. I just received your last letter. I feel it my duty to search my soul regarding my personal debt to you, as opposed to the perhaps larger debt to society, and to all the murdered unborn of the future ...

LARCH. Good one!

FUZZY. It is, frankly, hard for me to listen to my conscience and not turn you in to the authorities ... I suggest we cease all present communications ...

LARCH. *(At typewriter.)* Sincerely ...

LARCH and FUZZY. Doctor F. Stone ... *(Pause.)*

LARCH. Thank you, Fuzzy. You will be my perfect replacement. One who is acceptable to the authorities. You will also be my perfect lie. You will be on record as claiming to be against the very thing you shall continue to perform. You will play a role in life that is more strenuous than you ever could have been capable of. *(Fuzzy disappears.)* The fact that you died when you were eight years old is besides the point. *(Pause.)* Now. The only question is ... How will I get Homer Wells to play the part? *(Lights go down on him as Homer appears.)*

HOMER. After the harvest was over, Olive told Homer

OLIVE. With Wally gone back to school, I don't much like the idea of living here alone. I would like it very much if you could stay — if you thought you could be happy here. I like having someone in the house at night, and someone to talk to in the morning.

HOMER. Well I — *(Excited.)* I really like working on the farm.

OLIVE. Good!

HOMER. But I don't know — I'm not sure how Doctor Larch would feel about it.

OLIVE. Doctor Larch would like you to go to college one day. And so would I. I would be happy to inquire, at the high school in Cape Kenneth, if they'd work with you. You've had a very ... odd education.

HOMER. Yes.

OLIVE. Why don't you write and ask him. And I suppose, you should write to inquire about your medical condition too.

HOMER. My medical condition...?

OLIVE. To make sure if there's anything else you need to know. About your heart.

HOMER. My heart...?

OLIVE. Yes.

LARCH. Oh, good God!

HOMER. What about my heart?

OLIVE. You mean, Doctor Larch hasn't told you? *(Homer shakes his head.)* I'd drop him a note, if I were you. *(Homer exits.)*

LARCH. Dear Homer ... I do apologize for not telling you about your condition. Now, DON'T BE ALARMED! I would not even describe your heart as a condition, it is so slight. You had a fairly substantial heart murmur as a small child, but this had almost entirely disappeared when I last checked you — in your sleep. And I have delayed even mentioning your heart to you for fear of worrying you needlessly. *(Homer reenters, reading Larch's letter.)*

HOMER. You have (or had) a pulmonary valve stenosis, but

LARCH. PLEASE DON'T WORRY!

HOMER. It is nothing, or next to nothing.

LARCH. Aside from avoiding any situation of extreme stress or extreme exertion, I want you to know that you can almost certainly lead a normal life. *(Homer stops reading.)*

HOMER. A normal life? I am a Bedouin with a heart condition and you are telling me I can lead a normal life? I am in love with my best — and only — friend's girlfriend, but you tell me to try and avoid extreme stress?

LARCH. Now as to the other matter — we are deeply disappointed though of course we understand why you've decided to stay at the farm. But please — don't you forget where you belong. We're not getting any younger, you know.

HOMER. No, none of us is!

LARCH. While you are there and should you have a change of heart I'm sending along, under separate cover, your copy of *Grays Anatomy*, *Greenhills Office Gynecology*, and *The British Diseases of Women*. It's a masterpiece.

HOMER. God.

LARCH. And make sure to write — not only for MY sake, but for Nurse Angela and Nurse Edna so that they won't think you're just off somewhere having the time of your LIFE —

HOMER. *(Laughs.)* The time of my — okay. I'll write. I'll write! *(Homer exits.)*

LARCH. Damnit! Goddamnit! And then Doctor Larch went to the boys' division to check on *David Copperfield*, who'd had a fever when he'd gone to bed. *(He bends over* David Copperfield. *He hesitates, then kisses him. He goes next to him, kisses Snowy Meadows.)*

NURSE EDNA. Then, he kissed him. He went from bed to bed, kissing all the boys.

NURSE ANGELA. He didn't know all their names, but he kissed them anyway.

MRS. GROGAN. He kissed them all.

NURSE EDNA. I wish he would kiss ME.

MRS. GROGAN. I think it's nice.

NURSE ANGELA. I think it's senile. I think the old man is losing his marbles.

NURSE EDNA. I think it's the ether. He spilled some accidentally on his face this morning.

OLIVE. So then, it's settled then. You'll stay?

HOMER. I'll stay. Right. *(The company appears.)*

COMPANY MEMBER. In 194_, the city of Bath seemed dominated by the shipyards,

COMPANY MEMBER And by the ships that stood taller than the shipyard buildings,

COMPANY MEMBER. And by the bridge that spanned the Kennebec River.

COMPANY MEMBER. Bath was a workingman's town.

MELONY. As Melony soon discovered, it was too cold to keep looking for Homer Wells, so she got a job in the shipyards and began her winter employment on the assembly line

WOMEN WORKERS. Working with other women —

WALTER. And with an occasional handicapped man —

LORNA. On the first floor of a factory specializing in movable parts.

MELONY. The movable part to which Melony would devote her energies was a hexagonal-shaped sprocket. The sprocket arrived on the conveyor belt in front of her,

DORIS. Pausing there for exactly thirty-five seconds,

WALTER. Before it was moved on and replaced by a new sprocket.

FOREMAN WOMAN. The joint of the sprocket is packed with grease. You stick your finger in the grease, past the second knuckle. You insert six ball bearings into the joint. Push each ball bearing into the grease until you feel it hit bottom. All six should fit perfectly.

COWORKER The trick is to get only one hand greasy. That way, you can handle the ball bearings easier. *(Everybody gets to work. Melony tries.)*

MELONY. You could sit or stand. Melony tried both positions, alternating them through the day. She had a twelve-to-fourteen-second rest between sprockets, during which time she could look at the person on her left … *(She does.)*

DORIS. Her name was Doris. She had three children.

MELONY. One side of her face was still pretty,

DORIS. But the other was marred by a mole with whiskers in it.

MELONY. In the twelve to fourteen seconds Doris had between sprockets,

DORIS. She smoked.

MELONY. And at the person on her right …

WALTER. Walter.

MELONY. His problem was that —

WALTER. He could not pick up the ball bearings that he

31

dropped,

MELONY. And some of them got caught in the wheelchair apparatus,

WALTER. Which caused him to rattle —

MELONY. When he wheeled himself off for his coffee break or for lunch.

WALTER. Fucking ball bearings!

MELONY. One day, when the assembly line was —

FOREWOMAN. Reassembled!

MELONY. Melony got to be next to: *(Lorna appears.)*

MELONY. Who are you?

LORNA. I'm Lorna.

MELONY. I'm Melony. Are you new?

LORNA. Not as new as you.

MELONY. How long you been working here?

LORNA. About a year.

MELONY. A year! How do you stand it?

LORNA. There's worse jobs.

MELONY. Name one.

LORNA. Blowing bulldogs.

MELONY. I don't know about that. I'll bet every bulldog is different.

LORNA. Then how come every man is the same? *(Melony smiles. Lorna laughs. Sound of factory whistle.)*

FOREWOMAN. OK, everybody, clock in for graveyard shift. *(Lights go down on them. Lights up on Homer and Debra sitting in the "car," which is parked.)*

DEBRA. The Ferris wheel sure looks odd in the moonlight. Like a rocket launch.

HOMER. Yeah. Or the bones of some dinosaur.

DEBRA. Getting cold.

HOMER. I know. Soon it'll be too cold to go driving. Then what else will there be to do?

DEBRA. There's a Fred Astaire movie in Bath. Wanna go?

HOMER. Bath. That's almost an hour away. Maybe you should take somebody from your dancing class.

DEBRA. Don't you like Fred Astaire?

HOMER. Never seen him.

DEBRA. Well then.

HOMER. It's dancing I'm not so keen on.

DEBRA. But that's what Fred Astaire IS. I don't know what you've got against dancing.

HOMER. I don't know, either. *(Pause.)*

DEBRA. So what are you doing tomorrow night?

HOMER. Well, I was going to see Candy — she's home from Camden. And Wally did ask me to look after her.

DEBRA. You're going to see her without Wally?

HOMER. Right.

DEBRA. You're going to see her alone.

HOMER. Or with her dad.

DEBRA. Sure … *(Debra gets out of the car. Candy gets in.)*

CANDY. What do you want to do tonight?

HOMER. Your idea sounds fine.

CANDY. The Fred Astaire movie?

HOMER. That's great. I always wanted to see him.

CANDY. You don't mind the drive?

HOMER. It's less than an hour away. *(Sound of factory whistle. Lights up on Melony and Lorna on the assembly line, working side by side.)*

LORNA. I got married when I was seventeen. He was a garage mechanic, about twenty-one. He just married me 'cause I was the first person he slept with.

MELONY. Men. They're the worst.

LORNA. You're telling me.

MELONY. My boyfriend and I were doing swell until a rich girl came between us.

LORNA. What happened?

MELONY. He ran off with her.

LORNA. The bastard.

MELONY. But I figure one of two things has happened. Either he still hasn't fucked her, because she hasn't let him, and so he's figured out what he's missing. Or else she's let him fuck her — in which case, he's figured out what he's missing. *(Lorna laughs. Melony laughs. They look at each other.)*

LORNA. This overtime ain't bad, huh.

MELONY. Nope. *(Lorna drops a ball bearing down Melony's work*

33

shirt.)

LORNA. There's a Fred Astaire movie in town. You wanna see it? *(Lights go down on them. Lights up on Homer and Candy outside the movie theater.)*

A PATRON. *(To box office man.)* Two, please.

HOMER. When Homer Wells opened his wallet in front of the ticket booth, he realized that he'd never opened his wallet outdoors, in a winter wind, before. He put his back to the wind, but still the loose bills flapped.

CANDY. Candy cupped her hands on either side of his wallet,

HOMER. As if she were protecting a flame that was in danger of going out,

CANDY. And that was how she was in a position to catch —

HOMER. Her own treasured clump of pubic hair —

CANDY. When it blew free from Homer's wallet and caught on the cuff of her coat.

CANDY and HOMER. They both grabbed for it

CANDY. But Candy was quicker. *(She holds onto the clump of hair. Homer's hand closes on hers. They step away from the box office. Homer does not let go of Candy's hand.)* I'd like to take a walk.

HOMER. Right. *(They walk, Homer holding her hand. Sound of river. They stand.)*

CANDY. Perhaps you're a collector. Perhaps you're a pubic hair collector.

HOMER. No.

CANDY. This is pubic hair. And it's *mine*, right?

HOMER. Right.

CANDY. Only mine? You kept only mine?

HOMER. Right.

CANDY. Why? *(Pause.)*

HOMER. No doubt Homer Wells misunderstood the unfamiliar weight he felt upon his heart. What he felt was only love. But what he thought he felt was his pulmonary valve stenosis. *(Homer puts his hands to his chest. He has trouble breathing.)* I ... I ... *(Candy looks at him, suddenly upset.)*

CANDY. Is it your heart? Oh God, you don't have to say anything — please don't even think about it!

HOMER. My heart. You know about my heart?

CANDY. YOU know?!

HOMER. I ... I ...

CANDY. Don't worry!

HOMER. I love you ...

CANDY. Yes, I know. Don't think about it. Don't worry about anything. I love you, too.

HOMER. What? You DO...?

CANDY. Yes. Yes. And Wally, too. I love you AND I love Wally. But don't worry about it ...

HOMER. What...?

CANDY. Don't even think about it.

HOMER. Did Olive tell you about my heart?

CANDY. We all know about it.

HOMER. You DO...? *(Homer clutches his heart again.)*

CANDY. Don't think about it! Don't think about your heart, Homer!

HOMER. No...?

CANDY. Don't worry about me, or Wally, or any of it.

HOMER. What — what am I supposed to think about?

CANDY. Only good things. *(She looks at him.)* I can't believe you kept my hair!

HOMER. Well ...

CANDY. I mean, it's okay, I guess I understand. It, it may be peculiar, but it's certainly romantic.

HOMER. Romantic ... *(He holds Candy. Pause.)*

CANDY. Fog's rolling in. Guess we can see Fred Astaire dance another time. *(Lights go down on them. Sound of Fred Astaire-like music and singing.* Lights on the movie theater lobby. Melony walking out with Lorna. Mary Agnes Cork is also there, with her new parents, the Callahans. She goes up to Melony.)*

MARY AGNES. Hi.

LORNA. You talking to me, kid?

MARY AGNES. Hi. It's ME!

MELONY. Oh. Hi. So. You got out?

MARY AGNES. I've been adopted! That's Ted and Patty Callahan. They're in antiques. I'm Mary Agnes Cork Callahan.

MELONY. They let you keep your name?

---

* See Special Note on Songs and Recordings on copyright page.

35

MARY AGNES. I like my name. Besides, a Cork goes with a Callahan, don't it?

MELONY. This is my friend, Lorna.

LORNA. Hi.

MARY AGNES. Where's Homer?

MELONY. What?

MARY AGNES. Homer Wells. Isn't he with you?

MELONY. WHAT? Why?

MARY AGNES. I don't know. I just saw. I mean, those pretty people with the car ...

MELONY. WHAT car?

MARY AGNES. Well, it wasn't the same car, it wasn't the pretty car, but there was the apple on the door. I'll never forget that apple.

MELONY. What are you talking about?

MARY AGNES. I saw an old car, but it had that apple on it. I thought they was at the movie, those pretty people — and Homer, too.

MELONY. Where was the car?

MARY AGNES. What? I —

MELONY. Show me the car!

MARY AGNES. It's gone, now.

MELONY. What?

MARY AGNES. It's gone. It was right over there.

MELONY. Are you sure it was THAT apple? It had a double W, and it said Ocean View.

MARY AGNES. That's it. It just wasn't the same car, it was an old van, but I'd know that apple anywhere. You don't forget a thing like that.

MELONY. (Tiredly.) Oh, shut up ...

LORNA. What is it? Was your fella here with his rich cunt?

PATTY CALLAHAN. (To Mary Agnes.) Honey? Are you ready? (Mary Agnes starts off with her parents.)

MARY AGNES. I hope I see ya!

MELONY. What color was the van?

MARY AGNES. Green! I hope I see ya!

MELONY. (Yells.) You ever hear of an Ocean View?

CALLAHANS. No!

MARY AGNES. Can I see ya sometime?

36

MELONY. I'm at the shipyards. If you ever hear of an Ocean View, you can see me! *(Lights down on them. Lights up on Homer and Candy, sitting on the dock back at Heart's Haven.)*

CANDY. Is it okay?

HOMER. Is what okay?

CANDY. Your heart.

HOMER. I guess so.

CANDY. It'll be okay.

HOMER. What will be okay?

CANDY. Everything.

HOMER. Everything. Me loving you — that's okay. And you loving me, AND Wally — that's okay, too? *(Pause.)* Right ...

CANDY. I don't know what to do, either.

HOMER. We have to do the right thing.

CANDY. We have to — wait and see.

HOMER. I can be patient ... *(Lights up on Melony and Lorna. They are standing on the foggy banks of the Kennebec, holding beers.)*

LORNA. You don't know it was him. And you don't know if the rich cunt is still with him.

MELONY. No. I don't. I don't know anything at all, do I ... *(Lorna moves to Melony and touches her hand. Melony turns and looks at Lorna.)* Nothing ... *(Lights up on Homer, in bed, daytime, reading.)*

OLIVE. Homer!

HOMER. Yes?

OLIVE. Where is Pearl Harbor?

HOMER. What? *(A radio broadcast voice comes on as various groups gather to listen to it.)*

CANDY. You mean, with planes? From the sky?

RAY. Of course from the sky!

CANDY. How could they get away with an attack?

RAY. Because someone wasn't doing his job. *(More broadcast voice. Lights up on Lorna and Melony at the boarding house.)*

MELONY. We should just bomb Japan. No messing around. Just blow up the whole country. *(The members of the orphanage gather.)*

MRS. GROGAN. Where is Hawaii?

LARCH. Hawaii is in the Pacific.

NURSE EDNA. Oh, that's very far away.

LARCH. Not far enough.

NURSE ANGELA. There's going to be another war, isn't there?

LARCH. I guess it's already started. *(Sound of 1940s music. Wally dances on. He dances like Fred Astaire, only he puts on his flying uniform. The others are all by the radio. Wally freezes.)*

WALLY. Letter from Private First Class Wallace Worthington, Company A, Army Air Corps Division, Fort Meade, Maryland, to his mother Olive, dated January 6, 194_: Dearest Mother, It was wonderful being home for Christmas, 'specially since I'd only just enlisted two weeks ago. It now seems it's going to be more than a year before the Air Corps is going to teach me all I need to know in order to fly the plane that will carry the big bomb within me. *(Olive appears, reading the letter. Homer, Candy, and Ray also appear, holding their own letters.)* By that time, all the fighting will probably be over. Just my luck.

OLIVE. That *would* be lucky.

HOMER. Right!

WALLY. Ray, I've just finished putting together a pouch to hang above my bunk bed. It separates my shoe polish from my toothpaste, so I don't go using the wrong one on my feet.

RAY. Or in your mouth.

WALLY. Neat, huh Homer?

HOMER. Never mind toothpaste. Never mind shoe polish. What are they teaching you?

WALLY. The other fellows and I have been trying to come up with names for our airplanes, once we get them. I'm only just beginning. Candy, what do you think of Best Chance? Because, after all, you've got a better chance in a plane. *(He exits.)*

CANDY. A *chance?* Why would you want to be anywhere where all you get is a *chance?*

HOMER. It's all right, I think. A chance is enough. A chance is all we get, right? In the air, or underwater, or right here, from the minute we're born. Or from the minute we're not born, he thought.

CANDY. That's a pretty grim philosophy.

HOMER. Maybe. Maybe not. *(Pause.)* He told me ... Before he left — he asked you to marry him.

CANDY. He did? He told you?

HOMER. He said you wouldn't. He said, *(Wally reappears.)*
WALLY. She said she'd wait for me, but she wouldn't marry me.
CANDY. When did he tell you this?
HOMER. The night before. In our room. In the bedroom.
CANDY. And that's what he said I said?
HOMER. He said,
WALLY. She said she'd be my wife, but not my widow. What do you think of that?
HOMER. I think ... I don't know. What do you think?
WALLY. I understand, I guess. I mean, it is a war, after all. There's always a chance ... *(Wally exits.)*
HOMER. Is that what you call waiting and seeing? *(Pause.)*
CANDY. For years I've expected to be married to Wally. You ... you came along second. I have to wait and see about you. And now comes the war. I have to wait and see about the war, too.
HOMER. But you made him a promise.
CANDY. Yes. Isn't a promise like waiting and seeing? Did you ever make a promise, and mean it — *and* break it?
HOMER. Did I...? I ... *(Melony appears.)*
MELONY. Promise me, Sunshine.
HOMER. I promise.
CANDY. What? *(Melony disappears.)*
HOMER. Yes. I suppose I have ...
CANDY. And look how he ends it. Look what he says. *(She hands Homer the letter. He reads.)*
HOMER. Look after Homer. Look after his heart.
CANDY. But who's looking after my heart? Who's looking after mine?
HOMER. *(Moving to her.)* But that's what I mean. That's what I ...
CANDY. Shhh. *(Pause.)* I've got to go. Back to school. I'll be home next weekend. *(She puts a finger to his lips. She kisses him goodbye, lightly. Homer stands, wanting to extend the moment. Ray enters and sees this.)* Bye, Daddy!
RAY. Bye, honey ... *(Candy exits. Homer watches after her. Ray watches him, then says gently.)* Homer? Son?
HOMER. Hmn?
RAY. Pruning?
HOMER. Right ... *(Olive appears.)*

OLIVE. By spring, Wally was sent to Kelly Field, San Antonio, Texas, for Air Corps Cadet training

HOMER. Squadron 2, Flight C, *(Melony appears.)*

MELONY. And Melony knew it was time for her to hit the road again. *(Homer and Olive exit. Lorna appears and moves swiftly to Melony.)*

LORNA. You gonna work every winter and look for him every spring? You're lettin' a man make an asshole out of you.

MELONY. That's just what I'm not lettin' him do. *(Lorna hands her a present.)*

LORNA. This is for you.

MELONY. What is it?

LORNA. I used to knit.

MELONY. A child's woolen mitten —

LORNA. It's just the left hand. It was gonna be for a baby I never had, 'cause I didn't stay married long enough. I never got the right hand finished.

MELONY. The colors are very pretty. It's heavy.

LORNA. It's full of ball bearings. Swiped 'em from the shipyard. It'll make a super weapon. In case you meet anyone who's a bigger asshole than you are! *(Melony wipes away a tear. They embrace. Melony leaves. Lorna watches her go, then exits, as Homer, Mr. Rose, and the migrants appear on the cider house roof.)*

HOMER. That harvest, there was a ban on shore lights, and no Ferris wheel to watch at night …

MR. ROSE. It used to be over there — it was much higher than this roof, and brighter than all the stars if you hitched the stars all together …

MUDDY. It went round and round …

PEACHES. Now there's stuff out there, you said, Mister Rose?

MR. ROSE. Oh, yes. Under the ocean. Stuff with bombs. Underwater guns. And people.

JACK. There's people out there?

MR. ROSE. Lots of people. They got stuff so they can see you. They can see you anywhere. The world's changing, right, Homer?

HOMER. Right. It's all changing. It's all being invented.

MR. ROSE. Invented. And destroyed … *(Wally appears.)*

WALLY. Second Lieutenant Worthington! Merry Christmas! *(Olive,*

Ray, Candy, and Homer appear. Everyone cheers and applauds Wally.)
RAY. Say, Wally, you gonna have time to come see the Navy Yard in Kittery? We've been building torpedoes there for you boys!
WALLY. I've only got forty-eight hours, Ray.
OLIVE. Forty-eight hours! Isn't that ridiculous? That's not what I'd call coming home!
CANDY. Me neither. *(Wally hugs and kisses Candy, who hugs and kisses him back.)*
WALLY. *(To Homer.)* Hey, old pal. How's your heart?
HOMER. It's — it seems fine …
OLIVE. Forty-eight hours. Hardly any time at all … *(They freeze. Larch appears.)*
LARCH. Dear Franklin Delano Roosevelt … Merry Christmas! I know it's been a difficult year and that you must be terribly busy with the war yet I feel such confidence in your humanitarianism — and in your commitment to the poor, to the forgotten, and especially to children … You Roosevelts are national heroes! You are my heroes anyway. How can you tolerate this country's anti-American, anti-democratic abortion laws? What are you people thinking?
NURSE EDNA. Wilbur!
LARCH. You're not only crazy! You're ogres!
NURSE EDNA. Wilbur, the children can hear you! And the mothers! Everyone can hear you!
LARCH. No one hears me … *(They exit. The Heart's Haven scene unfreezes, as Wally shakes Ray's hand, then embraces Olive. She hugs him tightly.)*
OLIVE. Take care of yourself … *(They watch Wally go, then exit. Homer and Candy sit in the "car." Wally gets in the driver's seat.)*
HOMER. Do you want me to drive?
WALLY. Why?
HOMER. Maybe you want to hold hands.
WALLY. *(Laughs.)* We've already held hands. But thanks, anyway!
HOMER. So you've done it, you mean? *(Pause.)*
WALLY. What's that, old boy?
HOMER. I said, so you've done it? Had sex, I mean.
WALLY. Jesus, Homer. That's a fine thing to ask.
CANDY. Yes, we've done it. Had sex.

HOMER. I hope you were careful. I hope you took some precautions.

WALLY. Jesus, Homer!

CANDY. Yes. We were careful.

HOMER. Well, I'm glad. You should be. You should be careful — having sex with someone who's about to fly over Burma.

CANDY. Burma? *(To Wally.)* You didn't say where you were going. Is it Burma?

WALLY. I don't know where I'm going. Jesus, Homer, what's the matter with you?

HOMER. I love you both. If I love you, I've got a right to ask anything I want. I've got a right to know anything I want to know. *(They stop the "car.")*

WALLY. I don't know about you, Homer. You're becoming very philosophical.

CANDY. I would say eccentric. He's becoming very eccentric, in my opinion. *(He embraces Homer.)*

WALLY. I love you both, too, you know.

HOMER. I know you do. *(Wally embraces Candy, kisses her.)*

WALLY. Hey! I found a new name for my plane! This one I'm really gonna use. *Opportunity Knocks!* What d'you think?

HOMER. *Opportunity Knocks.*

WALLY. Catchy, huh? Bombs away! *(He waves and exits. Candy runs to him.)*

HOMER. Knocks. Knocks Once…? Twice…? Or just … Knocks … *(Homer and Candy walk.)*

CANDY. I'm sorry. But you don't have a right to know everything about me, whether you love me or not.

HOMER. Perhaps.

CANDY. Definitely.

HOMER. But all you've got to know is, do you really love him? Do you love Wally?

CANDY. I've grown up loving Wally. I have always loved Wally, and I always will.

HOMER. Fine. Then that's it, then.

CANDY. No. It isn't. Because I don't really even know Wally anymore. I — I know you better. And I love you, too. *(Homer sighs.)* What is it?

42

HOMER. Nothing. Just. Then we're in for more waiting and seeing, I guess. *(The company gathers.)*
COMPANY MEMBER. But were they?
COMPANY MEMBER. Shortly after apple blossom time,
COMPANY MEMBER. When the bees had spread their marvelous life energies through the orchards of Ocean View,
COMPANY MEMBER. Wally was sent to India. *(Sound of bomber plane.)*
WALLY. *OPPORTUNITY KNOCKS!!*
COMPANY MEMBER. Here were the headlines on the Fourth of July:
COMPANY MEMBER. YANKS WRECK RAIL BRIDGE IN BURMA,
COMPANY MEMBER. CHINESE ROUT JAPS IN HUPEH PROVINCE, *(The sound of bomber planes get louder. Wally, either suspended or disappearing upstage, shouts above the growing din of planes, bombing, and sirens.)*
WALLY.
There was a young man from Bombay
Who fashioned a cunt out of clay
But the heat of his prick
Turned it into a brick *(Sound out.)*
And chafed all his foreskin away.
(An explosion. Lights out on Wally. Lights up on Homer, working in the fields.)
HOMER. Homer Wells — beekeeper and orchardman — was mowing in the rows between the trees when the news came to him. Because the tractor was running, he didn't hear what Candy was yelling when she ran to him. *(Candy, from upstage, comes on, shouting.)*
CANDY. SHOT DOWN! SHOT DOWN! SHOT DOWN! *(She comes tearing over to Homer and into his arms.)*
HOMER. Wha...? What is it...?
CANDY. He was shot down — over Burma! *(She sobs. Homer holds her tightly.)*
HOMER. Wally ... Oh, Wally ... Over Burma ... *(Blackout.)*
COMPANY MEMBER. A month after Wally's plane was shot down, they heard from the crew of *Opportunity Knocks.*

43

COPILOT. Captain Worthington was nowhere to be found …

COMPANY MEMBER. In August, Burma officially declared war against Great Britain and the United States.

CANDY. Candy told Homer that she needed a new place to sit. The dock made her want to jump off. She'd sat too many times on that dock with Wally. It didn't help that Homer would sit there with her now.

HOMER. I know a place, Homer told her. *(He leads her to the cider house.)* Maybe Olive was right. Maybe they hadn't cleaned the cider house for nothing … *(Night. Homer and Candy walk to the cider house.)*

COMPANY MEMBER. That night in August, the trees were full, the boughs bent and heavy

COMPANY MEMBER. And the apples — all but the bright, waxy-green Gravensteins —

COMPANY MEMBER. Were a pale green-going-to-pink.

COMPANY MEMBER. The grass in the rows between the trees was knee-high;

COMPANY MEMBER. There would be one more mowing before the harvest.

COMPANY MEMBER. That night there was an owl hooting from the orchard called Cock Hill;

COMPANY MEMBER. Candy and Homer also heard a fox bark from the orchard called Frying Pan.

HOMER. Foxes can climb trees.

CANDY. No, they can't.

HOMER. Apple trees, anyway. Wally told me. What is it?

CANDY. The rain. Do you think it sounds as loud as that? Over there?

HOMER. I don't know.

CANDY. And the smell of the cider apples. It smells like the floor of the jungle … *(Homer enters the cider house, holding Candy. Night. Olive sits in Wally's room with the lights off.)*

OLIVE. If she married him … If she gave Wally up, and married him … How could I consider her unfaithful? I couldn't, no. It's just that, I know her. She wouldn't give Wally up without giving him up for dead … And neither Candy, nor I, believe that … He doesn't FEEL dead … There's a mosquito in here that's driving me

44

crazy. *(She turns on the lights.)* Where is it? Stupid mosquito. There must be terrible mosquitoes, where Wally is. Burmese mosquitoes … *(Night. Ray, sitting on his dock, slaps a mosquito on his neck.)*

RAY. Damn mosquitoes! Hell. They need to live, too, I guess. *(Pause.)* Look at that heat lightning … *(Pause.)* Poor Candy. Darling daughter. I know what you're going through. Don't let Wally stop your own life. If you lose him … let him go … Let him go, honey … And take the other fella … *(Pause.)* If it was me … I'd take the other fella … *(Night. Heat lightning flashes across the cider house.)*

CANDY. I think he's alive.

HOMER. I think he's dead.

CANDY. Look. The light's gone on in his room. *(Pause.)* He's alive. *(Homer touches her face.)*

HOMER. You're crying. *(He kisses her tears.)* I love you.

CANDY. I love you, too. But he's alive.

HOMER. He isn't.

CANDY. I love him.

HOMER. I know you do. I love him, too … *(Candy lowers her shoulders and puts her head against his chest. He holds her with one arm, and puts the other near her breast.)*

CANDY. *(Whispers.)* This is so hard … *(Olive gets up from Wally's bed, touches and smoothes it, pauses to look at the room, then turns out the light. She remains standing by the door. Flashes of heat lightning. Homer lowers Candy onto the bed in the cider house. They begin to make love.)*

RAY. If it were me, darling daughter … *(Homer and Candy make love, slow, with a moaning and needy, sad increasing. As they make love, Larch appears, dream-like, watching over their lovemaking.)*

LARCH. You say you love her. Then let her use you. It may not be the way you had in mind, but if you love her, you have to give her what she needs — and when she needs it, not necessarily when you think the time is right. And what can she give you of herself? Only what she has left … And if that's not everything you had in mind, whose fault is that? Are you not going to accept her because she hasn't got one hundred percent of herself to give? It's true … Some of her is over Burma. Are you going to reject the rest?

OLIVE. *(Praying.)* Oh, take pity on my son! Please! Please! Take

45

pity on my son! *(Homer and Candy reach climax. They kiss.)*
HOMER. I love you …
CANDY. I love you, too … *(Homer and Candy freeze. The lights change abruptly. The scene shifts as Larch remains onstage, and the nurses and Mrs. Grogan appear. Mrs. Grogan comes downstage holding pamphlets. They look out at the audience.)*
MRS. GROGAN. Anybody need these?
LARCH. Common misuses of the prophylactic
NURSE EDNA. One. Some men put the prophylactic on just the tip of the penis: this is a mistake, because the prophylactic will come off. It must be put over the whole penis, and it must be put on when the penis is erect.
NURSE ANGELA. Two. Some men try to use the prophylactic a second time: This is also a mistake. once you remove a prophylactic, throw it away!
MRS. GROGAN. Three. Some men take the prophylactic out of its wrapper: They expose the rubber to light and air for too long a time before using it. The rubber can dry out or develop cracks and holes. This is a mistake! Sperm are very tiny - they can swim through cracks and holes!
LARCH. Love is never safe. There is, in fact, no more safety to be found in love than there is to be found in a virus.
NURSE EDNA, NURSE ANGELA and MRS. GROGAN. It was Number Four of the Common Misuses of the Prophylactic that Homer Wells violated.
LARCH. Four. Some men stay inside their partners for a long time after they have ejaculated; what a mistake this is! The penis shrinks! When the penis is no longer erect, and when the man finally pulls his penis out of his partner, the prophylactic can slide completely off. Most men can't even feel this happening, but what a mess! Inside the woman you have just deposited a whole prophylactic
ENTIRE COMPANY. And all those sperm! *(Homer and Candy unfreeze.)*
HOMER. Uh-oh … *(The company disperses.)*
BIG DOT. Nearly three months after Wally's plane was shot down,
OLIVE. The harvest at Ocean View began.

46

CANDY. And Candy Kendall knew she was pregnant.

HOMER. They were working in the apple mart, *(Homer and Candy have reentered, carrying apple crates.)*

CANDY. Homer, what are we going to do...?

HOMER. Here, let me help you with that. *(Pause.)* We have to talk.

CANDY. Of course we have to talk. But not here. Not now. Besides, we have to wait and see.

HOMER. We don't have long to wait. We don't have long to see. *(Candy wobbles, nauseous.)*

BIG DOT. Homer, ain't you got no better manners than to watch a young lady puke? You just stay outside, darlin'. There's less fumes here. *(Candy starts to exit.)*

HOMER. Candy ...

BIG DOT. No one likes to be sick around the opposite sex, Homer.

HOMER. Right ... *(Big Dot moves upstage. Homer turns to Candy.)* What were you just trying to do?

CANDY. I don't know. Who knows? It's possible.

HOMER. What's possible?

CANDY. That if I work real hard ...

HOMER. You'll miscarry? What if I don't want you to miscarry?

CANDY. I'm not saying I WANT to —

HOMER. What if I want you to have the baby ...

CANDY. It's not your decision.

HOMER. It's my baby, too!

CANDY. But you're not HAVING it!

HOMER. And you mean you don't want the baby?

CANDY. I don't know if I want it or not.

HOMER. Why? Because you're ashamed?

CANDY. I'm not ashamed — of you! Or me! Or it!

HOMER. Then what?! What if I want you to marry me, and have the baby?

CANDY. Those are two different things!

HOMER. Why? Why do they have to be?

CANDY. Because they do!

HOMER. Because of Olive? It's because of Olive, isn't it?

CANDY. YES it's because of Olive. Okay?! Oh, Homer, it's just not the right — I'd marry you, AND have the baby, but what

47

would I tell Olive? How do we avoid telling her the truth? *(Pause.)*
HOMER. We'll find a way. *(Lights down on them. Lights up on Larch in the dispensary with Nurse Edna and Nurse Angela.)*
NURSE ANGELA. A WANTED BABY! We're going to have a WANTED BABY!
LARCH. If not a planned one. *(Nurse Edna reads the letter.)*
NURSE EDNA. "She's going to have my baby. Neither an orphan nor an abortion."
LARCH. And I suppose he's going to plant the damn trees.
NURSE EDNA. Finally.
LARCH. I knew he'd be back! He belongs with us!
NURSE ANGELA. Yes. He certainly does.
NURSE EDNA. I suppose we should get one of the rooms ready for them to sleep in.
LARCH. What are you talking about? Candy can sleep in the girls' division, and Homer can sleep where he used to sleep.
NURSE ANGELA. Doctor Larch, that's ridiculous!
NURSE EDNA. They're lovers, Wilbur! Surely they sleep together!
LARCH. Well, surely they *have* ... That doesn't mean that they have to sleep together here ...
NURSE EDNA. Homer said he was going to marry her.
LARCH. Going to!
NURSE ANGELA. I think it would be nice to have someone sleeping with someone else here ...
LARCH. It seems to me that we're in business because there's entirely too much sleeping together.
NURSE EDNA. They're lovers!
NURSE ANGELA. Nurse Edna said indignantly.
NURSE ANGELA and NURSE EDNA. And that decided it.
NURSE ANGELA. Candy and Homer would share a room with two beds on the ground floor of the girls' division.
NURSE EDNA. How they arranged the beds was their own business. *(Mrs. Grogan appears, followed by the girls' division.)*
MRS. GROGAN. Mrs. Grogan said she liked the idea of having a man in the girls' division.
MARY O'MALLEY. Occasionally, the girls complained of a prowler,

CAITLIN O'SHAUNESSEY. Or a peeping tom.

MEAGAN O'REILLY. Having a man around at night was a good idea.

MRS. GROGAN. Besides, I'm all alone over there — you three have each other.

LARCH. We all *sleep* alone over here.

NURSE EDNA. Well, Wilbur. Don't be so proud of it. *(They exit. Lights rise on the kitchen at Ocean View. Early morning. Olive sits with a cup of tea. Homer appears.)*

OLIVE. Almost ready?

HOMER. Yes. *(Pause.)* I hate to leave so close to the holidays. It's just, I think sooner might be better, for them, there. Doctor Larch isn't getting any younger. I should be of more use than I am here. With the harvest over, I don't feel I have enough to do.

OLIVE. You're a fine young man.

HOMER. Also. There's one more thing. Candy is coming with me. *(Pause.)*

OLIVE. Candy is a fine young woman. It is most unselfish of you both — when you could be enjoying yourselves — to give comfort and companionship to unwanted children. *(Pause.)*

HOMER. I could never thank you enough for everything you've done for me. *(Olive shakes her head.)* I'm so sorry about Wally.

OLIVE. He's just missing.

HOMER. Right. *(He puts his hand on her shoulder. They stay still for a long moment. Then, Olive rests her cheek on top of his hand.)*

OLIVE. You should take the white Cadillac ... *(Candy and Ray enter. Ray embraces Homer and Candy. Olive remains sitting at the kitchen table.)*

RAY. I think it's good for you both that you stick together. *(He hugs Candy and kisses her.)* And try and have some *fun!* *(Olive and Ray disappear as Homer and Candy begin their "drive." It starts to snow. The company appears around them.)*

COMPANY MEMBER. On their journey inland, the farther north they drove, the more the leaves had abandoned the trees.

COMPANY MEMBER. There was a little snow in Skowhegan, more snow in Blanchard and in East Moxie and in Moxie Gore,

COMPANY MEMBER. And they had to wait an hour in Ten Thousand Acre Tract where a tree was down, across the road.

COMPANY MEMBER. In Moose River and in Misery Gore, and in Tomhegan, too, the snow had come to stay.

COMPANY MEMBER. With the bad roads and the failing light and the snow that began to fall after Ellenville, it was already dark when they reached St. Cloud's. *(Two women appear, walking down the hill.)*

CANDY. Climbing the hill, the headlights of the white Cadillac

WOMAN 1. Illuminated two women walking toward the railroad station. One of them didn't have a scarf.

WOMAN 2. The other one didn't have a hat.

CANDY. The snow winked in the headlights as if the women were throwing diamonds in the air.

HOMER. May I give you a ride?

WOMAN 1. You're goin' the wrong way.

HOMER. I could turn around. *(Women disappear. Homer and Candy stand. They look at the orphanage.)* The snow falling in front of the light in the dispensary was the same kind of snow that had been falling the night that Homer arrived in St. Cloud's after escaping from the Drapers in Waterville. *(Homer and Candy stand there.)* Listen.

LARCH'S VOICE. *(Off. Reads.)* " ... Whether I shall turn out to be the hero of my own life, or whether that station will be held by anybody else, these pages must show ... " *(Homer clasps Candy's hand tightly. He rings the bell. Orphans, Nurse Edna, Nurse Angela and Larch appear and greet them.)*

NURSE ANGELA. And so Homer and Candy began to enjoy the life of a young married couple in St. Cloud's.

HOMER. He was in love —

NURSE EDNA and CANDY. And was loved —

HOMER. And he was expecting a child. What more is there?

LARCH. And he was

HOMER. Of use.

CANDY. All right, Margaret O'Reilly, time for your reading lesson.

MRS. GROGAN. *(To Nurse Angela and Nurse Edna.)* Isn't it wonderful? Candy's even teaching the slow ones how to read!

NURSE ANGELA. She talked to that couple who adopted Sally O'Malley this morning for an hour and a half! One would have

50

thought she was giving her own daughter up for adoption, the sweet girl!

NURSE EDNA. And she was wonderful with the other pregnant mothers yesterday. She calmed down that one abortion from Clarkstown by telling her all about her own!

NURSE ANGELA. Then she stayed with her practically all night, till she came out of the ether ...

NURSE EDNA. Oh, yes. She's a regular saint ...

LARCH. Homer. Scrub up, please. I need your help.

HOMER. What? What's the matter?

LARCH. I'm running behind because of that woman from Wainscott.

HOMER. A bad case?

LARCH. She'd already had the D without the C, you might say. She needed a completion curretage. Anyway, I need help with a C-section. A woman arrived this morning already in the second stage of labor — her membranes are ruptured — and the baby is breeched.

HOMER. Doctor Larch, I've already told you that while I'm here, I will not —

LARCH. This is a delivery, Homer.

HOMER. That's not the point —

LARCH. The woman might die. *(Pause. Homer scrubs up.)* Thank you. And afterwards, we'll go over today's pediatrics lesson.

HOMER. Why do I have to learn pediatrics?

LARCH. What if your baby turns out to be colicky?

HOMER. I'll put him on his stomach and rub his back.

LARCH. And what if he's hypertonic?

HOMER. I don't know, 'cause it'll never be quiet enough around here to make him less tense.

LARCH. I can see you've done your reading.

HOMER. Yes. And I know what to do about thumb sucking, crossed eyes, and diaper rash, too! It's amazing the number of things a baby can get!

LARCH. I wouldn't worry about yours. Candy seems a more than healthy specimen.

HOMER. *(Smiles.)* She does, doesn't she?

LARCH. Now then, no mooning! Let's get to work!

ORPHANS. It was the best Thanksgiving ever in St. Cloud's!

LARCH. Mrs. Worthington sent a whole case of champagne.

NURSE EDNA. *(Drunk.)* It's GOOD, Wilbur, isn't it.

ALL. At dinner, they had

ORPHANS. *(First half.)* A turkey

ORPHANS. *(Second half.)* And a ham.

LARCH. And Doctor Larch

HOMER. And Homer Wells

LARCH and HOMER. Had a

ALL. Carving contest.

ADULTS. Which everyone said

ALL. Homer won.

LARCH. He's quite a carver, our Homer. Of course, I wanted Homer to go to medical school, to be a doctor, to come back and relieve me here. But that's all right! Who wouldn't rather get a girl like you pregnant — and grow apples! *(He drinks. Then he whispers to Candy.)* Of course, he doesn't need to go to medical school to be a doctor *here*. There's just a few more procedures he ought to be familiar with ... Hell! Look at us! This isn't a bad place to raise a family. And if Homer ever gets around to planting the damn hillside, then you'll get to grow apples here, too! *(He winks at Candy and drinks.)*

HOMER. When Doctor Larch fell asleep at the table later that night, Homer Wells carried him back to the dispensary. *(Larch stirs in his sleep.)* Doctor Larch...? You all right...? *(Larch awakens slowly.)*

LARCH. Wha...? *(He sees Homer and extends his hand.)* Ah, Doctor Stone ...

HOMER. Doctor Who?

LARCH. Doctor Stone ... Fuzzy Stone, Fuzzy Stone, Fuzzy Stone ...

HOMER. Fuzzy ... Doctor Larch, I think maybe you should go back to sleep ...

LARCH. Of course, whatever you say, Doctor Stone ... I've been dreaming about you, Fuzzy.

HOMER. What IS all this about Fuzzy Stone? Fuzzy Stone died years ago ...

LARCH. The way you carved the turkey tonight. You haven't lost your touch.

HOMER. My touch?

LARCH. Your knife work. Very fine. *(Pause.)* How's the missionary work been going, Fuzzy? In India?

HOMER. Missionary work? India? I don't know what …

LARCH. How's your reading? Have you been studying the
Greenhill? And the *New England Journal of Medicine.* And *JAMA.*

HOMER. Listen to me. I'm not Fuzzy. And I'm not going to get
taken in by you, either.

LARCH. Taken in?

HOMER. I know what you're doing by bringing up all this doctor business. And it won't work.

LARCH. Homer, don't you see what is going on? Since you two
have come back, you're making a home for yourselves — and
Candy is happy here …

HOMER. We're not staying. We're only here until the baby
comes.

LARCH. If you stay, you can be a real married couple here.

HOMER. And have to live by your rules?

LARCH. Rules? What rules?

HOMER. The rules you make everybody here live by! And stop
talking to Candy behind my back! Telling her that I have a gift —

LARCH. You DO have a gift! A great one! And you are throwing
it away!

HOMER. By becoming a father? And an apple farmer! And
maybe a lobsterman?!

LARCH. You don't know the first thing about —

HOMER. I'm learning, goddamnit! I learned obstetrical procedure, right?! And the far easier procedure — the one that is against
MY rules!

LARCH. Selfish you are! When you won't even try and help the
women who have nowhere else to go!

HOMER. They come to YOU!

LARCH. And for how long?! Look at me, Homer. Look. Do you
really think I can keep going on like this forever? *(Pause.)* Listen to
me. You know who the doctor is!

HOMER. It's you! You're the doctor! *(Homer starts to exit scene
with Larch. Candy appears and goes to him.)*

53

CANDY. Maybe he's right.

HOMER. Who?!

CANDY. Doctor Larch. I mean, if you're really as good a doctor as he says you are —

HOMER. It's not about being good — it's about what I want! It's my life, not his!

CANDY. But what's wrong with this life? We like it here. And if we can raise a family …

HOMER. But I don't want to be here. If we go back to Ocean View —

CANDY. I'll have to face Olive.

HOMER. We've talked about it. We know what we'll say.

CANDY. Just think about it, Homer. Just THINK about staying. Okay? *(They exit. Melony climbs out onto a fire escape.)*

MELONY. On the fire escape of the apartment she shared with Lorna in Bath, Melony was awakened by the Kennebec, its ice beginning to grind downriver … *(Lorna appears.)* It's just the ice. *(Pause.)*

LORNA. Almost spring.

MELONY. Yes.

LORNA. You're not … gonna leave again, are you…?

MELONY. I …

LORNA. Please. Tell me no. *(Pause.)* If we're gonna be together, you gotta stop lookin' for him. Either you want him, or you want me.

MELONY. I want you.

LORNA. Good.

MELONY. But then, you …

LORNA. Yes?

MELONY. You. Don't ever leave me.

LORNA. I promise. *(They embrace.)*

MELONY. A permanent couple. An orphans' ideal.

LORNA. But Lorna wondered, if

MELONY. Melony stopped looking for Homer Wells …

LORNA. Would she stop thinking about him, too? *(Lights down on them. Lights up on Homer, outside, testing the ground. He works a spade into the frozen earth. Ray appears in Heart's Haven.)*

RAY. Dear Homer: As you requested, we're sending along the

baby trees. Your letter said you are planting a standard forty-by-forty. Olive is sending Half Macs, about ten percent Red Delicious, another ten or fifteen percent Cortlands and Baldwins. Oh, yeah, and a few Northern Spies, and some Gravensteins — Olive says, *(Olive appears, supervising the sending of the trees.)*

OLIVE. For apple pie. *(As Ray continues, the trees arrive, and Homer proceeds to plant.)*

RAY. You just better hope the ground unfreezes, and your back holds out. I'm building my very own torpedo, in the furnace room, under the lobster pound. Basically, it's just to see if I can do it. I guess I can. Of course, the hard part ain't the firing part — it's the guidin' it. Hard to believe it's been five months, please send my daughter my love. *(Homer stops to rest, leaning on his spade.)* Happy to know you'll both be back by blossom time. That's a nice time of year. Take care of yourself, and Candy ... Best, Ray ...

HOMER. It was the middle of April before Homer could dig the holes and plant the forty-by-forty orchard — which he did in three days. He'd wanted to plant the trees before Candy delivered. He wanted the hillside entirely planted when the baby was born. *(Larch enters.)*

LARCH. Almost done?

HOMER. Yes.

LARCH. You made it just in time.

HOMER. What do you mean?

LARCH. They're kind of scrawny, aren't they?

HOMER. They won't give much fruit for eight or ten years.

LARCH. Then I doubt I'll get to eat any of it.

HOMER. But even before there are apples on the trees, think how the trees will look on the hill.

LARCH. They'll look scrawny. Still, they're very evenly spaced. What did I do to make you so compulsively neat?

HOMER. Taught me surgery. *(Pause. Larch turns to go.)*

LARCH. You coming?

HOMER. Why?

LARCH. Candy's about to have her baby ... *(Homer throws down the spade and runs down the hill.)*

HOMER. What?! *(Larch lifts a finger.)*

LARCH. *I* deliver this one. Fathers are a bother in the delivery room. If you want to be there, just mind your own business ... *(Candy is wheeled in to the delivery room. Homer, on his way there, meets some of the orphans.)*

ORPHAN. What's she havin'?!

HOMER. Either a boy or a girl.

ORPHAN. What'll you name it?

HOMER. Well, Nurse Angela named me.

ORPHAN. Me, too!

HOMER. So if it's a girl, we're naming her Angela.

ORPHAN. And if it's a boy?

HOMER. If it's a boy, we'll call him Angel. That's really just Angela without the last A ...

ORPHAN. Angel?

HOMER. Right. *(Homer puts on his surgical mask.)*

DAVID COPPERFIELD. And will you leave it here?

HOMER. No.

ORPHANS. WHAT?!

HOMER. *(Pulling down his mask.)* No! *(He goes into the delivery room.)* It was hot in the delivery room.

NURSE EDNA. The warm weather had been unexpected. Because no one had put the screens on,

LARCH. Larch refused to open any windows. *(Nurse Angela is weeping through her mask.)*

HOMER. What's the matter with Angela?

NURSE EDNA. Candy told her about naming the baby after her.

NURSE ANGELA. Oh, Homer! *(She weeps, embracing him.)*

LARCH. Angela, come right back here!

NURSE ANGELA. Sorry!

LARCH. And change your mask again.

NURSE EDNA. *(To Homer.)* This is already her second. *(They proceed.)*

HOMER. Anything I can ...

LARCH. No, Homer, but thank you. *(Homer paces.)*

ORPHANS. Homer? Homer? What's happening? *(He runs out.)*

HOMER. Shh! Everything's fine! I'll let you know! *(He runs back.)*

NURSE ANGELA. As the baby's head emerged,

LARCH. A drop of Larch's sweat baptized the child squarely on its temple —

NURSE EDNA. — literally before it was entirely born —

HOMER. And Homer Wells could not help thinking that this was not unlike David Copperfield being born with a caul. *(Pause.)* What about the shoulders? Where are the shoulders?

LARCH. I've got it covered, Homer.

HOMER. Okay, I just thought —

CANDY. I can't. I can't.

NURSE EDNA. Relax, darling, you're doing fine ...

LARCH. When the shoulders did not follow quickly enough to please Larch, he took the chin and occiput in both hands and drew the infant downward until,

NURSE EDNA and NURSE ANGELA. In a single, easy, upward motion,

LARCH. He delivered the posterior shoulder first.

HOMER. Homer Wells, biting his lip, nodded his approval as the anterior shoulder — and the rest of the child — followed. *(Larch holds the baby up.)*

NURSE EDNA. It's an Angel! *(Homer runs out.)*

HOMER. It's a boy!

BOYS. HOORAY! *(Everyone applauds. Nurse Angela bursts into fresh tears and turns away.)*

NURSE EDNA. Only after the placenta was born did Doctor Larch say, as he sometimes did,

LARCH. Perfect!

NURSE EDNA. Then, as he had never done before, *(Larch kisses Candy, through his mask. The nurses hand Angel to Homer. He holds him.)*

HOMER. Hello, Angel ... Welcome ... Welcome to the world ...

NURSE EDNA. Eight pounds, seven ounces!

NURSE ANGELA. And neither an orphan nor an abortion ... *(They exit. Lights up on Ocean View. Olive sits at the kitchen table, an unopened telegram in her hand. Ray comes through the door.)*

RAY. There you are, Olive. I thought you might like to come over to the basement and see the torpedo. I just finished it ...

OLIVE. Ray.

RAY. What is it?

OLIVE. This. *(She holds up the unopened telegram.)*

RAY. What's it say?

OLIVE. I haven't opened it yet. Postman left just three minutes ago. I've been sitting here.

RAY. You want me to...?

OLIVE. No. Now you're here. I will. *(She opens the telegram. Reads to herself.)* Oh, my God. My God. My God.

RAY. Is he ... *(She hands the telegram to Ray. He reads it.)* Jesus. *(Lights down on them. Homer and Larch in the orchard.)*

HOMER. I've been thinking about my heart, Doctor Larch.

LARCH. What about it, my boy?

HOMER. I've been thinking I'd like to know more about it.

LARCH. Like what?

HOMER. Like what's wrong with it. It might be useful. It might be helpful not just for me, but for Candy and Angel, too. *(Pause.)*

LARCH. I see. Well, I understand, of course. But the thing about your heart, Homer, is ... *(Candy bursts in.)*

CANDY. Homer! Homer!

HOMER. Candy?

CANDY. This just arrived. *(She extends her hand. A telegram. Homer takes it. Reads.)*

HOMER.
Wally found alive/stop/
recovering encephalitis Ceylon/stop/
liberated from Rangoon Burma/stop/
temperature ninety two degrees/ stop/
weight one hundred five pounds/ stop/
paralyzed/stop/
love Olive

(Pause.) A hundred and five pounds.

CANDY. *(Whispers.)* Alive ...

HOMER. Paralyzed.

LARCH. Encephalitis. *(Pause. Homer and Candy look at each other.)*

LARCH, HOMER, CANDY, RAY, and OLIVE. Alive ... *(Snow starts to fall.)*

HOMER. It was thirty-four degrees in St. Cloud's when Homer Wells went to the railroad station and dictated a telegram to Olive.
God bless you and Wally/stop/
when will we see him/stop/

Candy and I home soon/stop/
I have adopted a baby boy/stop/
love Homer
(Homer and Candy stand together, hand in hand, the baby in their arms.)

CURTAIN

ACT TWO

The company gathers.

ENTIRE COMPANY. Fifteen years!

HOMER. For fifteen years, Homer Wells had taken responsibility for the writing and posting of the cider house rules. *(To Mr. Rose.)* I hope they don't offend anyone. They're just little rules.

MR. ROSE. Yes. They are.

HOMER. But it does concern me that no one seems to pay attention to them.

MR. ROSE. We got our own rules, too, Homer.

HOMER. Your own rules.

MR. ROSE. 'Bout lots of things. 'Bout how much we can have to do with you, for one thing.

HOMER. With me?

MR. ROSE. With white people.

HOMER. I see.

MR. ROSE. No, you don't. You DON'T see — that's the point.

HOMER. How's your little girl?

MR. ROSE. She growin', like your boy.

HOMER. And how's your lady?

MR. ROSE. She lookin' after the little girl.

ENTIRE COMPANY. Fifteen years!

CANDY. And for fifteen years, Homer and Candy had made their own rules, too. Even before Wally came home.

HOMER. They were standing in the cider house after they'd returned to Heart's Haven

CANDY. *(To Homer.)* How do you feel?

HOMER. Like an orphan. How do *you* feel?

CANDY. I won't know until I see him.

HOMER. What will you know then?

CANDY. If I love him, or you, or both of you. Or else I won't

60

know any more than I know now.

HOMER. Do you mean that you won't ever know if you love him or me?

CANDY. It may be all confused by how much he's going to need me.

HOMER. You don't think I'll need you, too?

CANDY. We'll have to wait and see. *(Pause.)*

HOMER. Past a certain point, I won't wait.

CANDY. What point is that?

HOMER. When Angel is old enough to either know he's an orphan or know who his parents are. I won't have Angel thinking he's adopted.

CANDY. Let's agree to something.

HOMER. Okay.

CANDY. Whatever happens, we share Angel.

HOMER. Of course.

CANDY. We both get to be his parents. Regardless of what happens. We both get to live with him. We get to be his family. Nobody ever moves out.

HOMER. In the same house? Even if you go with Wally?

CANDY. Like a family.

HOMER. Like a family. *(Candy picks up a baby and holds it in her arms. Wally appears in a wheelchair.)*

WALLY. Candy and Wally had been married less than a month after Wally returned to Ocean View. Wally weighed one hundred and forty-seven pounds

HOMER. And Homer pushed the wheelchair down the church aisle.

OLIVE. Olive Worthington had died in Cape Kenneth Hospital before the war was over, even before they'd sent Wally home.

NURSE CAROLINE. Cancer. Inoperable. Spreading quickly. Nothing to be done.

OLIVE. In the end, Olive thought Wally had come home. In their last few visits she mistook Homer for Wally. *(While Homer wheels Wally, Olive takes him by the arm, stopping him.)* You must forgive him.

HOMER. Forgive him?

OLIVE. Yes. He can't help how much he loves her, or how much he needs her. He's an orphan.

HOMER. Who is?

OLIVE. HE is. Don't you forget how needy an orphan is. He's come from having nothing. When he sees what he can have, he'll take everything he sees. My son, don't blame anyone. Blame will kill you.

HOMER. Blame will kill you …

RAY. Ray Kendall had died shortly after Wally and Candy were married. He was killed when his lobster pound blew up. His whole dock was blown apart, and his lobster boat sank. He'd been tinkering with his homemade torpedo.

CANDY. Candy regretted that she'd not told her father about Homer and Angel Wells. It was no consolation to her that she imagined Ray already knew everything.

RAY. She had been able to understand, by his silences, that he'd wanted to hear it from her.

HOMER. Blame will kill you. Dread remorse.

ENTIRE COMPANY. Fifteen years!

COMPANY MEMBER. For fifteen years they were a couple:

MELONY and LORNA. Lorna and Melony.

MELONY. Melony was handy. She had learned electricity at the shipyards where she was one of a staff of three electricians.

LORNA. Lorna became more domestic. They rarely fought because Lorna would not fight back. In fifteen years, she had discovered that Melony relented if there wasn't a struggle. Given any resistance, Melony would never quit.

MELONY. You don't fight fair.

LORNA. You're much bigger than I am.

MELONY. The way that Melony liked to fall asleep was with her big face on Lorna's tight bare belly.

LORNA. In fifteen years, there was only one night when Lorna had to ask her to move her heavy head before she had soundly fallen asleep.

MELONY. What is it? You got cramps?

LORNA. No. I'm pregnant. *(Pause.)*

MELONY. Let me understand this. We've been like a married couple for fifteen years, and now you're pregnant. I guess what you're telling me, is that when women are fucking each other, it takes a lot longer for one of them to get pregnant than when a woman is fucking some guy. Right? Like about fifteen years — like THAT long!

LORNA. Please don't go. Don't leave me.

MELONY. I'm packing up YOUR things. I'm not the one who's pregnant. I don't have to go nowhere.

LORNA. Don't throw me out. It was just a guy. Just one guy — and it was just once!

MELONY. You take the train to St. Cloud's. When you get there, you ask for the orphanage.

LORNA. I ask for the orphanage? *(Train whistle.)*

MELONY. *(Handing a box to Lorna.)* And you give this to an old woman named Grogan — if she's still alive. Don't say nothing, just give it to her. And if she's dead, bring the carton back. *(Pause.)* I was faithful to you. I was loyal as a dog.

LORNA. Please don't throw me out.

MELONY. I hope you have a real monster inside you. I hope it tears you to pieces when they drag it out your door. Fifteen years!

ENTIRE COMPANY. Fifteen years! *(The box appears at St. Cloud's.)*

MRS. GROGAN. What is it?

LARCH. Well, go on, open it. I haven't got all day.

MRS. GROGAN. Who left it?

NURSE ANGELA. Someone named Lorna. I never saw her before.

LARCH. Me neither. *(They take out a huge Army surplus coat. Hood. Fur collar.)*

NURSE EDNA and NURSE ANGELA. Heavy. Nice. *(Mrs. Grogan tries it on.)*

MRS. GROGAN. Lots of secret pockets. Probably for weapons and mess kits.

LARCH. Or the severed arms and legs of enemies.

MRS. GROGAN. I don't get it. *(She takes out loose change and bills and counts it. Suddenly:)* Oh, my God! It's been, it's got to be, fifteen years! More! Oh, that dear girl!

NURSE EDNA and NURSE ANGELA. Who?

MRS. GROGAN. MELONY!! *(Larch takes out copper wire from another pocket, along with wire-cutters.)*

LARCH. I'll bet she robbed some electrician.

NURSE ANGELA. A BIG electrician.

NURSE EDNA. You two. It's a warm coat, at least it'll keep her warm.

LARCH. It'll give her a heart attack, lugging it around.

NURSE CAROLINE. I can wear it.

LARCH. Who are you?

NURSE CAROLINE. Her name was Caroline,

HOMER. Homer Wells had met her at Cape Kenneth hospital, where he and Candy had volunteered during the war, and she was nice to the patients and tough to the doctors.

NURSE CAROLINE. Hospitals aren't perfect, they're just expected to be. And doctors aren't perfect either; they just think they are.

HOMER. Right.

NURSE CAROLINE. Homer Wells has sent me here.

LARCH. Sent you for what?

NURSE CAROLINE. I'm a trained nurse. I'm here to help you.

LARCH. Help me do what?

NURSE CAROLINE. I believe in the Lord's work.

LARCH. Well, why didn't you say so?

NURSE EDNA and NURSE ANGELA. She was constantly of use *(Caroline puts on the coat.)*

LARCH. Nurse Caroline, you are — well, somewhat REMI-NISCENT of Melony ... if Melony had been a Marxist. And an angel ...

ENTIRE COMPANY. Fifteen years!

HOMER. For fifteen years, Homer Wells kept records: The number of times he'd made love to Candy since Wally had come home: 270.

CANDY. What Homer didn't know was that Candy also kept a record. 270, written on the back of the photo of her teaching Homer how to swim. 270 times in fifteen years.

HOMER. 270 times! That's an average of eighteen times a year, only one and a half times a month ...

CANDY. And they'd agreed that for the sake of the family, they would never get caught.

HOMER. They knew Wally would have accepted what HAD happened.

CANDY. It was what was happening NOW that they knew Wally would want to know

CANDY and HOMER. And they couldn't tell him.

HOMER. And they had another reason to be careful.

WALLY. I can still aim the gun, and the gun still goes off, and it still goes off with a bang — for me. It's just that no one ever finds the bullet.

ENTIRE COMPANY. Fifteen years!

COMPANY MEMBER. That autumn, the autumn of 195_,

HOMER. Was the autumn Angel Wells was fifteen. *(Angel Wells enters.)*

ANGEL. He was learning how to drive Candy's car.

CANDY. I taught your father how to swim. I guess I can teach you how to drive.

ANGEL. Of course Angel knew how to drive all farm vehicles, too. He knew how to mow, how to spray, and how to operate a fork-lift. Great!

COMPANY MEMBER. That autumn,

LARCH. In 195_,

NURSE EDNA, NURSE ANGELA and NURSE CAROLINE. Wilbur Larch was ninety-something,

LARCH. And sometimes his face would hold so still under the ether cone that the mask would stay in place after his hand dropped to his side. *(Larch takes out the black bag.)* But Larch still had plans for the future of his orphanage. *(He looks at newly inscribed lettering on the old bag.)* F.S. Fuzzy Stone. *(He starts to wrap the bag, as if to mail it.)*

COMPANY MEMBER. That autumn,

MELONY. Melony, finding herself alone again, took out an old newspaper article and photograph she had framed

MARY AGNES. In a frame she had bought from Mary Agnes Cork.

WALLY. The article was about Captain Worthington, and the picture —

MELONY. Which Melony had recognized, fifteen years ago —

WALLY. Was also of Wally. The article was all about the miraculous rescue of the downed and paralyzed pilot, who had been awarded the Purple Heart.

MELONY. Melony liked the picture, and the part of the article that said Wally was a local hero,

WALLY. A Worthington who for years owned and managed

MELONY. *(Reads.)* The Ocean View Orchards in Heart's Haven ... *(Pause.)*

ENTIRE COMPANY. Worthington. *(Pause.)* Ocean View. *(Pause.)* Heart's Rock. *(Pause.)* Fifteen years!

MELONY. Are you still there, Sunshine?

MR. ROSE. That autumn Mr. Rose wrote to Wally 'bout bringin' the daughter. My daughter. And her daughter. Mr. and Missus Worthington.

CANDY. Candy.

WALLY. Wally.

MR. ROSE. And Mr. Wells.

HOMER. Homer. And you're...?

ROSE ROSE. Rose.

HOMER. We know that's your last name, what's your first name.

ROSE ROSE. Rose is my first name.

CANDY. Rose ROSE?

ROSE ROSE. Rose Rose.

WALLY. And what's HER name?

MR. ROSE. Haven't thought of a name for her yet. Still thinkin' it out.

HOMER. That's a good idea. *(Rose Rose and Mr. Rose exit.)*

WALLY. It's sure been a while since we've seen her.

CANDY. I think she must be about Angel's age.

HOMER. Right. *(Wally hits Homer with a jab. Homer falls to the floor, surprised.)*

CANDY. Wally!

WALLY. I'm so SICK of it! *(Pause.)* It's time you learned a new word, Homer.

CANDY. Jesus, Wally.

HOMER. I'm okay.

WALLY. I'm sorry. It just gets on my nerves. You saying "right" all the time. *(Wally forgets and raises himself to help Homer. He starts to fall. Candy goes and grabs Wally by the arms. She hugs him, chest to chest, and Homer springs up and helps put Wally back in his chair.)*

WALLY. I'm sorry, buddy. *(He puts his head on Homer's shoulder.)*

HOMER. It's okay, Wally. Everything's okay. *(They exit as Rose Rose appears, washing her hair over a bucket. Her naked back is to us.)*
ANGEL. *(Off.)* Hello?
ROSE ROSE. Is that you? *(Angel enters. He isn't wearing a shirt.)*
ANGEL. Oh. I'm sorry. *(She turns, jumps and covers herself, her hair all wet.)* Sorry. I should have knocked.
ROSE ROSE. That okay. I thought you were …
ANGEL. I … wondered if I could help you get anything for your baby. Good morning.
ROSE ROSE. You must be Angel. *(Angel looks at her, smitten.)*
ANGEL. Yes.
ROSE ROSE. Baby sleepin' now. But she seem to be teethin'.
ANGEL. My dad said. He thought you might need some pacifiers.
ROSE ROSE. She kind of cranky today.
ANGEL. Wish I'd worn a shirt.
ROSE ROSE. Why?
ANGEL. More formal, I guess.
ROSE ROSE. No. Your tan look nice. *(Angel smiles and relaxes a little.)* What this for?
ANGEL. The bourbon? You dab it on Baby Rose's gums. It numbs them.
ROSE ROSE. Yeah? You make her drunk.
ANGEL. No, I won't. It'll just put her gums to sleep.
ROSE ROSE. These here pacifiers. They better than a bottle?
ANGEL. With a bottle, Baby Rose would keep sucking air through the hole, and she'd start burping or getting a gassy stomach.
ROSE ROSE. How come you know so much?
ANGEL. I just.
ROSE ROSE. How old are you?
ANGEL. Almost sixteen. How 'bout you?
ROSE ROSE. 'Bout the same. If you be a good doctor, you be my hero for today. *(Angel smiles at her. Mr. Rose appears.)*
MR. ROSE. Gotcha! *(He grabs Angel.)* Hey, Angel. How you doin'? You still growin', I think. *(To Rose Rose.)* I used to carry him on top of my head. He used to grab them apples I couldn't reach!
ANGEL. I'm counting on growing a little more. *(Pause.)* Well. I'll see ya later.
MR. ROSE. That right, Angel. Just remember, I gotcha! *(Angel*

leaves.)

ANGEL. But it was Rose Rose who'd really gotten him.

CANDY. Where are you going all excited?

ANGEL. To my room. To get my dictionary.

CANDY. Dictionary? For what?

ANGEL. To find girls' names. *(Out.)* How else do you impress a girl who hasn't been able to think of a name for her baby? *(Angel puts on a cap. Company begins to gather. The harvest.)*

WALLY. God, I love the harvest! It's my favorite time!

ANGEL. *(Looking through the book.)* Abby? Alberta? Amanda? Amelia? Aurora? ... Aurora Rose ... God, no.

CANDY. *(To Angel.)* Where are you going in my hat?

ANGEL. It's MY hat.

HOMER. *(To Angel.)* Hey, it's cold this morning — put on a shirt!

ANGEL. I got to warm up the tractor!

HOMER. Warm yourself up first!

ANGEL. Edith? Esmeralda? Eve! *(He bumps into Herb.)*

HERB. Watch where yer goin'.

ANGEL. Felicia! Francesca! Frederica!

HERB. Asshole.

BIG DOT. No, that's you. You're the asshole, Herb. *(Pause.)* Hey Squeeze, how many more apples we got?

SQUEEZE LOUISE. Half a crate left.

BIG DOT. May as well finish this before lunch.

SQUEEZE LOUISE. Okay. *(Melony approaches Big Dot.)*

MELONY. Does a guy named Homer Wells work here?

BIG DOT. He sure does. *(To Herb.)* Where's Homer?

HERB. He's fixing the tractor out in the Frying Pan.

SQUEEZE LOUISE. *(Looking her over.)* Are you a pal of Homer's?

MELONY. I used to be. I haven't seen him in a while.

FLO. You just come to say hello?

MELONY. Actually I come for work. I done a lot of pickin'.

HERB. We already got enough pickers.

BIG DOT. Just go tell Homer there's someone to see him. Homer's the boss. *(Herb exits.)*

MELONY. The boss?

BIG DOT. If you're gonna work here, you may as well know it. That guy who was just here is the number-one asshole.

MELONY. There's just one? *(Squeeze and Big Dot laugh.)*

FLO. Tell us how you know Homer Wells.

BIG DOT. From where and since when?

MELONY. From St. Cloud's, since forever. He was my guy. *(Pause.)*

SQUEEZE LOUISE. Your guy. Really.

BIG DOT. You don't say ... *(Homer and Angel are fixing the "tractor.")*

HOMER. Boy, when I was your age — in St. Cloud's — it was really tough to beat off with any privacy. *(Pause.)*

ANGEL. Really.

HOMER. Yup. You know, I was the oldest, I guess I was about your age. And I was supposed to be in charge of all the other kids. I knew they weren't old enough to have pubic hair, or to know what to make of their little hard-ons.

ANGEL. *(Laughs.)* So how'd you manage it?

HOMER. I waited till I thought they were all asleep.

ANGEL. Twelve boys? Was it a long time?

HOMER. You have no idea. *(They laugh.)* Hand me that wrench, will you?

ANGEL. This one?

HOMER. The smaller — that one. There was one kid, I think the first time he did it, when he actually squirted — when he ejaculated, you know — he thought he'd hurt himself.

ANGEL. *(Laughs.)* You're kidding! *(They laugh. Pause.)*

HOMER. Of course I tried to explain it all to him. It was hard to make him understand that he hadn't done anything wrong. Because it's natural. It's perfectly healthy and normal. But these things have a way of, you know ... getting distorted ... *(Pause.)* This kid. You know. He didn't realize. It was only natural that he would have feelings about girls ... about sex ... long before he'd have the opportunity to do anything about it. *(Pause.)* After all. *(Pause.)* Is there anything you'd like to ask me? About anything? *(Pause. Angel laughs. Then he stops.)*

ANGEL. Why don't you have a girlfriend? Why don't you even seem interested? *(Pause.)*

HOMER. This was not the question Homer had expected. Still ...

(Pause.) I had a girlfriend. In St. Cloud's. She was something of a bully. Older than me, and stronger.

ANGEL. *(Intently.)* No kidding.

HOMER. We weren't very much alike. It was a case of, you know, the sex happening before there was a friendship ... or there really being no friendship ... and after a while, there wasn't any sex anymore, either.

ANGEL. So what happened after that?

HOMER. After that, well ... I met Wally and Candy. Tell him, Homer thought. Tell him everything. Tell him now. *(Pause.)* I suppose ... I would have married Candy, if she hadn't married Wally. I mean, she was almost my girlfriend. For about five minutes. That was when Wally was in the war, when we wondered if he was still ... I've always been close to Candy and Wally, and then — once I had you — I started to feel that I already had everything I wanted. *(Pause.)*

ANGEL. So you still kind of like Candy? I mean, you're not interested in anybody else?

HOMER. Kind of. Have you met anybody you're interested in?

ANGEL. Um. Well. Sort of. But I don't know if she ...

HOMER. Really? Who?

ANGEL. *(Laughs.)* Nah ...

HOMER. *(Laughs.)* Who?! *(He pokes Angel in the ribs. Angel rolls on his side, poking back at Homer. Homer grabs Angel in a headlock. They wrestle. They laugh. Herb approaches.)*

HERB. Hey, Homer! If you quit dickin' around, I got a message for you. There's a fat woman who's at the mart, lookin' for work. She says she knows you.

HOMER. Knows me?

HERB. Says she wants to be a picker, and she asked for you. She knows you. *(Homer gets slowly to his feet.)*

ANGEL. A fat woman, huh? I guess you didn't tell me about HER ... *(He pokes Homer. Pause.)* Pop? Who's the woman? *(Homer starts buttoning his shirt in a panic.)* It can't be the bully, can it? *(They get on the tractor.)*

HOMER. Half a trailer of apple crates still needed to be unloaded, but Homer drove too fast, dumping an occasional crate.

ANGEL. They had an empty trailer in no time.

HOMER. And on the way back, Homer took the public road instead of winding through the back orchards.

ANGEL. *(Shouts.)* Do you think it's her? He stood with his hands on his father's shoulders,

HOMER. His feet braced against the trailer hitch.

ANGEL. You gotta admit, it's a little exciting! *(Melony, Big Dot, Squeeze appear. Homer sees Melony and approaches her. Angel whispers.)* It IS her, isn't it?

HOMER. Hello, Melony.

MELONY. How you doin', Sunshine?

BIG DOT. Sunshine! *(Pause. Melony stares at Angel.)*

MELONY. There's no doubt about who YOU are. You look more like your father than your father. *(Pause.)*

HOMER. It's nice that you see a resemblance. But my son is adopted.

MELONY. Adopted? *(Candy appears, chewing an apple. She walks between Homer and Angel.)*

CANDY. Hi!

HOMER. This is Melony. This is Mrs. Worthington.

CANDY. How do you do?

MELONY. Mrs. Worthington? *(She looks from Angel to Candy, and from Angel to Homer. Wally appears, wheeling himself.)*

WALLY. *(Cheerily.)* Isn't anybody working today? Oh, hello!

MELONY. Hi.

CANDY. This is my husband.

MELONY. Your husband?

HOMER. *(Mumbles.)* This is Mr. Worthington.

WALLY. Everybody calls me Wally.

HOMER. Melony and I were in the orphanage together.

WALLY. Really? That's great. Get them to show you around. Show her the house, too. Maybe you'd like to take a swim? And please stay for the first press tonight. *(Candy almost chokes, but swallows hard. Wally starts to wheel himself off.)* Dot? Get me a count of the number of bushels of Gravs we have. I got a phone order waiting …

BIG DOT. Meany will know, he was just in there …

WALLY. Then someone get Meany to tell me … *(Melony watches Wally go.)*

71

ANGEL. Would you like to see the pool first?

MELONY. Well, I don't swim, but it would be nice to see it.

CANDY. I'll show you the house, after Angel's shown you the pool.

HOMER. I'll show you the orchards.

MELONY. You don't have to show me no orchards, Sunshine. I seen lots of orchards before.

HOMER. Oh.

ANGEL. Angel showed her the pool.

CANDY. Sunshine. *(Homer watches after them.)*

HOMER. She knows.

CANDY. What?

HOMER. Everything.

CANDY. You told her?

HOMER. Course not. She just knows. She always knows.

ANGEL. I could probably save you. If you fell in.

MELONY. Incredible.

ANGEL. I could teach you how to float, I bet.

MELONY. Just incredible.

CANDY. Candy showed her the downstairs;

MELONY. Nice place ya got.

HOMER. Homer showed her the upstairs.

MELONY. Boy, you really done all right for yourself. Mind if I use the bathroom?

HOMER. No, of course not. It's right upstairs. *(To Candy and Angel.)* The both of you, just go back to work. I need to talk to her ALONE.

ANGEL. She's exciting. She might do anything.

HOMER. EXACTLY. *(Candy and Angel exit.)*

MELONY. In the bathroom, Melony began ejecting razor blades from a crude metal dispenser. *(Melony cuts her finger.)* Shit! Then she saw a cigarette lighter. She used the lighter to melt the handle of Homer's toothbrush, sunk the razor blade in the softest part and waited for the handle to harden. *(Pause.)* Quite a nice little weapon. *(Looks at herself.)* She saw her face reflected in the mirror. The mirror had never been Melony's friend. *(She weeps.)* She threw the toothbrush back into the sink and left it there. *(She leaves the bathroom and goes to Homer, who stands alone. Pause.)*

HOMER. Everything all right?

MELONY. I somehow thought you'd end up doin' somethin' better than ballin' a poor cripple's wife and pretendin' your own child ain't your own.

HOMER. *(Surprised.)* What? ... It's not quite like that.

MELONY. I got eyes. I can see what it's like. It's like SHIT. It's ordinary, middle-class shit. Bein' unfaithful and lyin' to the kid. You of all people!

HOMER. You don't understand.

MELONY. Don't I? I had you figured all wrong. I always thought you'd end up like the old man.

HOMER. Like Larch?

MELONY. I figured you for that. You know, the missionary. The do-gooder with his nose in the air.

HOMER. I don't see Larch quite that way.

MELONY. Don't be snotty to me! You got your nose in the air — I got that part right. But you ain't exactly no missionary. You're a creep!

HOMER. Thanks a lot!

MELONY. What, you think I get my rocks off embarrassin' you? Do you think I was always lookin' for you only to give you a bad time?

HOMER. I didn't know you were looking for me.

MELONY. Well, I ain't anymore! You knocked up somebody you shouldn't a been fuckin' in the first place, and you couldn't even come clean about it to your own kid. Ain't that brave? In my book, Sunshine, that's a creep!

HOMER. Where you going? Melony? Melony? *(She leaves. Homer watches her go. Wally, Candy, Angel enter, go to supper table.)*

WALLY. I thought she was staying for supper.

ANGEL. I thought she wanted a job.

CANDY. Why would she want to pick apples?

ANGEL. Maybe she just wanted to look you over, Pop!

WALLY. *(Laughs.)* I bet your dad never told you about Debra Pettigrew!

CANDY. Oh, come on, Wally, that wasn't serious.

ANGEL. You left something out, Pop!

WALLY. We used to double-date. Your old man usually got the

73

backseat.

CANDY. Come on, Wally!

WALLY. You should have seen your old man at his first drive-in. He didn't know what drive-ins were for!

CANDY. Maybe Angel doesn't know what they're for!

ANGEL. Of course I know what they're for!

WALLY. Of course he knows what they're for!

HOMER. Only Bedouins don't know. *(Sound of car horn.)*

ANGEL. There's Petey Hyde!

CANDY. You going driving AGAIN?

ANGEL. Through all the orchards! It's a game!

HOMER. No driving after dark, young man, remember! Not after the apple crates have been put out! *(Angel runs off. Homer calls after him.)* REMEMBER! *(Pause.)*

WALLY. Well. Think I'll go to the pool. Looks nice in the twilight. *(He wheels himself off slowly. Pause.)*

HOMER. It's time to tell.

CANDY. No, please.

HOMER. It's time to tell everyone everything. No more waiting and seeing. *(Candy goes to him and holds him, hugging him, but he fails to respond.)* I'll work it out with you. Any way you want to do it. *(She hugs him hard. He turns away from her.)*

CANDY. We'll talk later. Please. I'll see you by the pool.

HOMER. We can't talk about this around the pool.

CANDY. I'll meet you at the cider house.

HOMER. That's not a good idea.

CANDY. While everybody's at the first press. Just take a walk! You walk there your way, I'll walk there my way! We'll meet! Goddamn it! *(Wally wheels himself back in. Homer and Candy freeze.)*

WALLY. It's so nice out. I thought — *(To Candy.)* Maybe you'd like to take a drive.

CANDY. A drive?

WALLY. A quick spin. What's wrong with your lip?

CANDY. Nothing.

WALLY. It's bleeding.

CANDY. I bit it, accidentally.

WALLY. Hard, looks like.

CANDY. Tell you what. You boys go. I'll finish the dishes.

74

WALLY. What do ya say, old boy? *(To Candy.)* Can we take your jeep?

CANDY. Nice night for it. And keep down the top. *(Candy exits. Homer and Wally drive in the "jeep.")*

WALLY. You know what I miss?

HOMER. (Walking? Loving your wife?)

WALLY. What's that?

HOMER. Nothing. What. What do you miss?

WALLY. Flying. I really miss flying. I miss being up there. Above everything. That's how it was.

HOMER. I never did it.

WALLY. That's right. My God! You've never flown. We've got to — and Angel — he'd find it exciting. It's the — it's the — thing I miss most. *(Pause. Wally reaches across the "gear shift" and "pops it" into neutral.)* Cut the engine a second. Let's just coast. *(Homer turns the key.)* Cut the headlights, too. Just for a second. *(Homer does.)*

HOMER. For just a moment, they seemed to be completely lost, possibly plunging off they knew not where. *(Pause. Homer turns the "headlights" back on.)*

WALLY. That was flying. *(Pause. They drive. They stop.)* Don't ever think I'm not grateful to you, for all you've done, old boy.

HOMER. Come on.

WALLY. No, I mean it. I know how much you've done for me, and I rarely get the opportunity to say how grateful I really am.

HOMER. You've certainly done everything for me, Wally.

WALLY. It's not the same, old boy. Believe me, it's not the same at all. *(Wally wheels himself off.)*

HOMER. On his way to the cider house, Homer was struck by the sight of a package waiting for him in the apple-mart office. *(He opens the package. It is the leather doctor's bag.)* The leather was scuffed and soft, and the brass clasp was so tarnished that its luster was as dull as the cinch buckle of an old saddle. But the gold initials were bright and new. *(Homer reads.)* F.S. *(Fuzzy appears.)*

FUZZY. Hello, Doctor.

HOMER. Fuzzy?

FUZZY. Hello, Doctor Stone. *(Larch appears.)*

LARCH. Doctor Stone.

HOMER. Doctor Stone. *(Fuzzy and Larch disappear. Candy is*

waiting for Homer in the cider house. She lights a candle by a made bed. Homer appears, carrying the doctors' bag.)

CANDY. What are you carrying?

HOMER. This. It arrived today from Doctor Larch. *(Candy opens the bag.)*

CANDY. Gravensteins?

HOMER. I put them in. *(He takes the bag back, holding it.)* The thing about a good doctor's bag. Is that it's comfortable to carry. *(Pause.)* I'm sorry. We've tried it — we've certainly tried — but it just doesn't work. Only the truth will work.

CANDY. What truth? That we've been betraying Wally? That all those years ago we pretended to adopt a baby from St. Cloud's and brought him back here? That for fifteen years we've raised our own baby to think it was born an orphan?

HOMER. We did it, remember, for Olive's sake, remember?

CANDY. We lied …

HOMER. For a while.

CANDY. For fifteen years. Angel will hate me.

HOMER. Angel will never hate you.

CANDY. Do you really think he's old enough to know all this?

HOMER. He's old enough to beat off, he's old enough to know what drive-ins are for. I think he's old enough.

CANDY. Oh, Homer. *(He goes to the bed and puts his hand on top of hers. She takes his hand and puts it under her dress. He doesn't pull away.)* Do you think Wally will throw me out?

HOMER. If he did, I wouldn't. Then you'd be with me. That's why he won't.

CANDY. What will Angel do?

HOMER. What he wants.

CANDY. Where will you go?

HOMER. Will I have to go anywhere? *(Mr. Rose heard, off.)*

MR. ROSE. Rose? That you? *(Candy scrambles into the shadows. Mr. Rose appears. He seems slightly drunk.)* Rose?

HOMER. Evening, Mr. Rose.

MR. ROSE. Homer?

HOMER. Hello.

MR. ROSE. I was looking for my daughter.

HOMER. She's not here. She — she was going to the first press

76

with Angel, I think.

MR. ROSE. Right. They probably out for a drive. *(He sees a figure in the shadows. Candy senses she's caught. She appears.)* Mrs. Worthington ...

CANDY. Hello, Mr. Rose. We were just making sure everything was okay down here.

MR. ROSE. Oh. Of course. That's mighty kind. *(Pause.)* What's in the bag, Homer?

HOMER. Apples.

MR. ROSE. That would be strange. You the apple doctor?

HOMER. *(Laughs.)* Right.

CANDY. Well then.

HOMER. We'll take our leave.

MR. ROSE. You coming to the first press, too?

CANDY. Oh, we'll be there!

MR. ROSE. Good. Then we'll see you in a little bit. *(They leave. He starts out, then turns. Sees something. He picks up the candle nub. Pockets it. He exits. Sound of a jukebox. Melony comes on, eating pizza.)*

MELONY. Melony, who had hitchhiked from Bath to Ocean View, hitchhiked back on the same day. She went to the pizza bar where everyone went,

LORNA. And she was looking so woebegone that Lorna left the lout she was with and sat down at the bar next to her. *(Pause.)* I guess you found him.

MELONY. He's changed.

LORNA. She told Lorna the story.

MELONY. It wasn't for ME that I felt so bad. I mean, I didn't really expect him to run away with me, or anythin' like that. It was just him. He was really better than that, I thought. He was someone I thought was gonna be a hero. I guess that's dumb, but that's what he looked like — like he had hero stuff in him.

LORNA. You don't know everythin' that's happened to him. *(Bob comes over.)*

MELONY. I guess what's the matter with Homer is that he's a man. I only ever met one who didn't let his dong run his life. And he was an ether addict.

BOB. Are you with me, or have you gone back to her?

77

MELONY. Cool it, Bob. We was just talkin'. She was just bein' an old friend.

BOB. I thought you was on vacation. Why doncha go somewhere where there's cannibals?

MELONY. Why doncha go beat off in a bucket? Why doncha go try to fill a pail. Go drip in a teaspoon.

BOB. Bob twisted her arm too sharply.

MELONY. He broke it.

LORNA. Then Bob broke her nose against the formica counter

WORKERS. Before some of the shipyard workers pulled him off her.

LORNA. Lorna took her friend to the hospital,

HOSPITAL WORKER 1. And when they'd put the cast on her arm

HOSPITAL WORKER 2. And had set her nose —

MELONY. They set it almost straight —

LORNA. Lorna took Melony back to the women-only boarding-house,

LORNA and MELONY. Where they both agreed they belonged: together. *(They embrace.)*

LORNA. How come you're not gonna press charges against Bob?

MELONY. Suppose it works?

LORNA. Pardon me?

MELONY. Suppose they really put Bob in jail, or send him off somewheres? Then when I'm better, I won't be able to find him.

LORNA. Oh. *(Lights down on them. Mrs. Grogan appears.)*

MRS. GROGAN. The next day in St. Cloud's, a terrible thing occurred. *(Nurse Edna, Nurse Angela and Nurse Caroline rush in with a woozy woman on a gurney.)*

NURSE EDNA. WILBUR!

NURSE ANGELA and NURSE CAROLINE. DR. LARCH!

LARCH. What's the matter?

NURSE CAROLINE. I helped her walk up the hill. She'd gotten off the train on the wrong side of the tracks.

LARCH. What's wrong with her?

NURSE EDNA. We don't know.

NURSE ANGELA. She won't tell us.

NURSE CAROLINE. Her temperature is a hundred and four.

LARCH. My God. She's burning up.

NURSE ANGELA. The poor girl. She's skin and bones.

LARCH. How many months is she? How many months are you? Six? Seven? *(Woman gasps and breathes heavily.)* I'm going to have to look inside you. *(Woman gasps.)* No, really, I'm not going to hurt you. I'm just going to look. *(He bends to look.)*

WOMAN. It wasn't me. I would never have put all that inside of me.

LARCH. All that? All what?

WOMAN. It wasn't me. I would never do such a thing.

LARCH. Doctor Larch bent so close to the speculum, he had to hold his breath.

NURSE EDNA. The smell of sepsis and putrefaction was strong enough to gag him if he breathed or swallowed,

LARCH. He just kept looking and marveling at the young woman's inflamed tissue.

NURSE EDNA. It looked hot enough to burn the world.

NURSE CAROLINE. Doctor Larch. Doctor Larch!

LARCH. Through the speculum, he felt her heat against his eye.

NURSE ANGELA. Blood pressure is dropping.

NURSE EDNA. The woman had come to them unidentified,

NURSE ANGELA. Pulse is very weak.

NURSE EDNA. Bringing only her burning infection,

NURSE CAROLINE. Her overpowering discharge,

LARCH. Her dead but unexpelled fetus,

NURSE EDNA. And several of the objects she — or someone else — had put into herself in order to expel it. *(Pause.)* God, so much blood. She's bleeding so much.

LARCH. Her punctured uterus. *(The woman writhes slowly, moaning incoherently.)*

NURSE CAROLINE. Acute peritonitis.

NURSE ANGELA. We're losing her, Doctor Larch.

NURSE CAROLINE. Her unstoppable fever.

NURSE ANGELA. There's no heartbeat!

NURSE CAROLINE. She reached Doctor Larch too late,

NURSE ANGELA. For him to save her ... *(Larch starts CPR with a closed-fisted thump on the woman's chest.)*

LARCH. Dear God ... I should be able to save her. I CAN —

NURSE ANGELA. It was too late, she was too far gone ...

LARCH. Damnit — GODDAMNIT —

NURSE CAROLINE. Don't blame yourself.

NURSE EDNA. You mustn't ... You tried, Wilbur.

LARCH. She was alive when she got here. I'm supposed to be the doctor.

NURSE CAROLINE. Then BE one, and stop being maudlin. *(Larch stops trying to revive the woman.)*

LARCH. I'm too old. Someone younger, quicker, might have ...

NURSE CAROLINE. You're not seeing things as they are ...

LARCH. Aren't I? *(He moves to the dispensary.)* I've had it, ladies. I'm finished. It's time for me to be replaced. And I don't want to leave it up to the board. Or to old age. Or to ether. It's time to take my chances with Homer Wells ... *(He goes into dispensary.)*

NURSE EDNA. What's he going to do?

NURSE ANGELA. I have no idea.

NURSE CAROLINE. If he can hold himself responsible for a case like this, then he IS too old ...

NURSE EDNA. But he's not incompetent!

NURSE ANGELA. No, but once he starts thinking he is, he's had it ... *(Nurse Edna goes to dispensary door.)*

NURSE EDNA. Wilbur? Listen to me, please. You're NOT too old. You're NOT incompetent. You're NOT too old ...

LARCH. But Wilbur Larch couldn't hear her. He was too busy writing a letter. He told Homer everything. He told him about Fuzzy Stone. He did not beg. He said he was sure Angel would accept his father's sacrifice. He'll value your need to be of use ...

Here is the trap you are in, Homer. Because abortions are illegal, women who need and want them have no choice in the matter, and you — because you know how to perform them — have no choice, either. If abortion was legal, you could feel free not to do it because someone else would. But the way it is, you're trapped. Women are trapped, and so are you.

You are my work of art. Everything else has just been a job ... I don't know if you've got a work of art in you, but I know what your job is, and you know what it is, too. You're the doctor. *(Pause. Larch exits, as Angel, Rose Rose and Baby Rose get on the "tractor," which Angel drives standing up.)*

ROSE ROSE. Why you wear that old baseball cap?

ANGEL. What?

ROSE ROSE. You got nice eyes, but nobody see 'em. You got nice hair, but nobody see it. And you got one pale forehead, 'cause the sun can't find your face. If you didn't wear that dumb cap, your face would be as brown as your body. *(Angel takes the cap off and tosses it away.)*

ROSE. Why you do that?

ANGEL. I thought you didn't like that hat.

ROSE ROSE. I didn't like that hat on YOU ... *(Angel stops the "tractor," jumps down and retrieves the cap. He jumps back on and puts it on her head. Rose Rose smiles at him, pleased.)* You better be careful. You don't wanna get involved with me.

ANGEL. *(Laughs.)* How old ARE you, anyway?

ROSE ROSE. 'Bout your age.

ANGEL. How do you like the name Gabriella?

ROSE ROSE. I never heard it before.

ANGEL. Gloria?

ROSE ROSE. That nice. Who it for?

ANGEL. Your baby. I've been thinking of names for your baby.

ROSE ROSE. Why you thinkin' of that?

ANGEL. Just to be of use. To help you make up your mind.

ROSE. Thank you. But I don't know as we need your help.

MUDDY. You countin' me, Angel?

ANGEL. I got you.

MUDDY. Ain't you a checker?

ANGEL. Sure, I got you!

MUDDY. Don't you wanna check me then? Better make sure I ain't pickin' pears, or somethin'. *(Angel gets down from tractor and goes to look at Muddy's bushel. Muddy suddenly takes Angel by the arm.)* You don't wanna go into the knife business with Mistuh Rose.

ANGEL. What? *(Muddy turns and walks away. Angel watches him go. He gets back on the tractor.)* Are you still together, you and the father?

ROSE ROSE. Baby got no father. I wasn't ever TOGETHER. *(Pause.)*

ANGEL. I like Hazel and Heather. They're both names of plants, so they sort of go with Rose.

ROSE ROSE. I don't have no plant, I got a little girl.

ANGEL. I also like the name Hope.

ROSE ROSE. Hope ain't no name.

ANGEL. Well, how about plain old Jane? *(She touches him, putting her hand on his hip.)*

ROSE ROSE. Don't never stop. I never knew there was so many names. Go on.

ANGEL. *(Excited.)* Katherine? Kathleen?

ROSE ROSE. Go on.

ANGEL. Mabel? That means lovable. Malvina? That means smooth snow.

ROSE ROSE. I never livin' where they got snow. You can go on with them names, any time …

ANGEL. One morning —

ROSE ROSE. When it was so cold that Rose Rose had left Baby Rose with Candy —

ANGEL. Angel saw that she was shivering and gave her his sweatshirt.

ROSE ROSE. She wore it all day.

ANGEL. She was still wearing it when Angel went to help with the cider press that night, *(Sound of whooping.)*

ROSE ROSE. But in the morning she was wearing one of Mr. Rose's sweaters. *(To Angel, giving him his sweatshirt back.)* He say it okay if I wear your hat, but for you to wear your own shirt.

ANGEL. Is there something wrong with your eye, Rose? Is that a … *(Rose Rose pulls the cap down even lower over her eyes.)*

ROSE ROSE. I told you. You don't wanna get involved with me. *(She starts off.)*

ANGEL. Wait. If you're frightened …

ROSE ROSE. What?

ANGEL. If you need a place … If you're frightened about staying in the cider house … you can always stay with me. With us. There's an extra bed in my room, or I could leave altogether and we could make it a guest room for you and Baby Rose.

ROSE ROSE. A guest room? *(She laughs.)* Angel. You are the nicest man I ever knew. *(She turns away again.)*

ANGEL. Let's go to the beach.

ROSE ROSE. What?

ANGEL. Let's take a drive. To the beach.

ROSE ROSE. What for?

ANGEL. To swim! The ocean! The saltwater!

ROSE ROSE. I don't know how to swim.

ANGEL. You don't have to swim to enjoy the ocean. You don't have to go in over your head.

ROSE ROSE. I don't have no bathin' suit.

ANGEL. You got to at least let me take you to see it! *(He tugs her by the arm. She cries out. He takes his hand away from her back and sees blood.)* My God.

ROSE ROSE. It's my period. *(Pause.)* Let's just sit here for awhile. *(Pause. Carefully, Angel puts his arms around her. They kiss.)*

ANGEL. After they kissed for a while,

ROSE ROSE. She showed him some of the wounds — not the ones on the backs of her legs, and not the ones on her rump —

ANGEL. He had to take her word for those.

ROSE ROSE. She showed him only the cuts on her back.

ANGEL. They were fine, thread-thin, razorlike cuts. They were extremely deliberate, very careful cuts that would heal completely in a day or two. They were slightly deeper than scratches. They were not intended to leave scars. *(Rose Rose kisses him, hard.)*

ROSE ROSE. I told you. You shouldn't have no business with me. I ain't really available.

ANGEL. Angel agreed not to bring up the matter of the cuts with her father,

ROSE ROSE. That would only make things worse —

ANGEL. Rose Rose convinced him of that. *(Rose Rose exits. Angel goes to the kitchen where Homer, Wally and Candy have gathered.)*

HOMER. He cut her?

WALLY. He deliberately cut her?

ANGEL. No doubt about it. I'm a hundred percent sure.

HOMER. I can't imagine how he could do that to his own daughter.

CANDY. We have to do something.

WALLY. We do?

CANDY. Well, we can't do nothing!

WALLY. People do.

ANGEL. If you speak to him, he'll hurt her more. And she'll

know I told you.

CANDY. I wasn't thinking of speaking to him. I was thinking of speaking to the police. You can't carve up your own children.

HOMER. But will it help her — if he gets in trouble?

WALLY. Precisely. We're not helping her by going to the police.

ANGEL. Or by speaking to him.

HOMER. There's always waiting and seeing.

ANGEL. I could ask her to stay with us. She could just stay here, even after the harvest.

CANDY. But what would she do?

HOMER. There aren't any jobs around. Not after the harvest.

WALLY. It's one thing having them pick. I mean, everyone accepts them. But they're only migrants. They're supposed to move on. I don't think that a colored woman with an illegitimate child is going to be made to feel all that welcome in Maine.

CANDY. Wally, this isn't the South. In all the years that I've been here, I've never heard anyone object.

WALLY. Let one of them actually try to live here and see what happens.

ANGEL. Please. She needs our help. Or we could do it your way. We could wait and see. *(Angel gives Homer a look and leaves. Homer watches him go.)*

HOMER. He's in love with the girl.

WALLY. As plain as the nose on your face, old boy. Where have you been? *(Wally exits. Mr. Rose, Angel and Rose Rose appear.)*

HOMER. The next day, Homer asked Mr. Rose to meet him on the cider house roof,

MR. ROSE. While below them, Angel tried to teach Rose Rose how to ride a bicycle.

ANGEL. Now pedal. Now pedal.

ROSE ROSE. I can't!

ANGEL. Not so fast! Don't pedal so fast!

ROSE ROSE. I can't help it! *(Rose Rose and Angel exit. Homer and Mr. Rose watch.)*

HOMER. She seems unable to balance the bicycle and pedal it at the same time.

MR. ROSE. Yes, Homer. To balance, and pedal, AND steer simultaneously looks to me like a distant miracle.

HOMER. It's the kind of thing you're supposed to learn when you're a little kid, I guess.

MR. ROSE. Can you ride one?

HOMER. I never tried. It doesn't look easy.

MR. ROSE. I never tried, either. *(Shouts heard, off.)*

HOMER. You remember what you said to me, once, about the rules?

MR. ROSE. What rules?

HOMER. You know, those rules I put up every year in the cider house. And you mentioned that you had other rules — your own rules for living here.

MR. ROSE. Yeah. Those rules.

HOMER. I thought you meant that your rules were about not hurting each other — about being careful. Sort of like my rules, too, I guess.

MR. ROSE. Say what you mean, Homer.

HOMER. Is someone getting hurt? I mean, this year — is there some kind of trouble? *(Shouts heard, off.)*

MR. ROSE. She fallen off now.

HOMER. It looks like she's trying to hurt herself. Deliberately.

MR. ROSE. Why would she be doing that? *(Pause.)*

HOMER. I'm asking about someone being hurt. I'm asking. About the rules. *(Pause. Mr. Rose reaches into his pocket, and takes out the burned-down nub of a candle. Homer sees it. Homer closes his fingers around the candle. Mr. Rose pats his hand.)*

MR. ROSE. That 'gainst the rules, ain't it? *(Shouts heard, off.)* She slipped all right. Looks like she got herself a cramp. *(Pause.)* What about them rules? *(Homer puts the candle in his pocket. He and Mr. Rose regard each other. Mr. Rose leaves. Homer goes to Candy, who is working in the kitchen.)*

CANDY. He's not admitting to anything.

HOMER. Of course he's not.

CANDY. But is he doing it?

HOMER. Yes, I think so, yes.

CANDY. Well what are we going to —

HOMER. He knows. About us.

CANDY. Of course he knows. But we can't let that stop us. We have to help her, what can we —

HOMER. *(Angry.)* I don't know! *(Frustrated, he goes. Larch appears.)*

LARCH. When Homer returned to the apple-mart office,

NURSE CAROLINE. He found some mail waiting for him on the counter. *(Homer reenters, looks at the mail.)*

HOMER. A letter from Melony. *(He tears it open. Melony appears.)*

MELONY. Dear Sunshine, I thought you was going to be a hero. My mistake. Sorry for hard time. Love, Melony.

HOMER. And a letter from Doctor Larch.

LARCH. You are my work of art. Everything else has just been a job. I don't know if you've got a work of art in you, but I know what your job is, and you know what it is, too. You're the doctor.

HOMER. And one from Nurse Caroline.

NURSE CAROLINE. Don't be a hypocrite. I hope you recall how vehemently you were always telling me to leave Cape Kenneth, that my services were more needed here — and you were right. And do you think your services aren't needed here, or that they aren't needed right now? Things here are terrible! And just who do you think the board's going to replace him with if you don't step forward?

HOMER. Any doubts in Homer's mind that were remaining about the doctor's bag with the initials F.S. engraved in gold had disappeared with the darkness just before dawn. *(He goes to writing table.)* He sent a single, short note, addressed to them both. The note was simple and mathematical. One. I am not a doctor.

HOMER and LARCH. Two. I believe the fetus has a soul.

HOMER, LARCH, and NURSE CAROLINE. Three. I'm sorry. *(Homer exits.)*

LARCH. Sorry? He says he's SORRY?!

NURSE ANGELA. Of course, he isn't a doctor. There'll always be something he'd think he didn't know. He'd always be thinking he was going to make an amateur mistake.

LARCH. That's why he'd be a good doctor! Doctors who think they know everything are the ones who make the most amateur mistakes!

NURSE CAROLINE. So what do we do?

NURSE EDNA. We wait and see.

LARCH. Not me. Homer can wait and see. But not me! *(He goes to the typewriter.)* He sat at the typewriter in the dispensary. He wrote this simple, mathematical note to Homer Wells.

One. You know everything I know, plus what you've taught yourself. You're a better doctor than I am — and you know it. Two. You think what I do is playing God, but you presume you know what God wants. Do you think that's not playing God? Three. I am not sorry — not for anything I've done (one abortion I did not perform is the only one I'm sorry for). I'm not even sorry that I love you. *(He walks.)* Then Doctor Larch walked to the railroad station and waited for the train. He wanted to see the note sent on its way. *(Stationmaster appears.)*

STATIONMASTER. Later, the stationmaster,

LARCH. Whom Larch rarely acknowledged,

STATIONMASTER. Admitted he was surprised that Larch spoke to him.

LARCH. But because Larch spoke after the train had gone,

STATIONMASTER. The stationmaster thought that Larch might have been addressing the departed train.

LARCH. Goodbye. *(Stationmaster disappears.)* He walked back up the hill to the orphanage.

MRS. GROGAN. Would you like some tea, Doctor Larch?

LARCH. I'm feeling too tired for tea. I want to lie down.

NURSE CAROLINE. Nurse Caroline

NURSE EDNA. And Nurse Edna

NURSE EDNA and NURSE CAROLINE. Were picking apples,

NURSE CAROLINE. And Larch went a little way up the hill to speak to them.

LARCH. You're too old to pick apples, Edna. Let Caroline and the children do it.

NURSE CAROLINE. He then walked a short distance with Nurse Caroline, back toward the orphanage.

LARCH. If I had to be anything, I'd probably be a socialist, but I don't want to be anything. Frankly, I'm just too tired. *(Pause.)* Then he went into the dispensary, and closed the door. *(The stage clears, but for Larch. He goes and sets up the ether apparatus, as he describes, slowly, what he is doing.)* Despite the harvest weather, it was still warm enough to have the window open during the day.

He closed the window, too. It was a new, full can of ether. Perhaps he jabbed the safety pin too roughly into the can, or else he wiggled it around too impatiently. *(He inhales.)* Suddenly, he was traveling. But where?

CONDUCTOR. New England Express! Now arriving, South Station, Boston! *(Music plays. Mrs. Eames appears.)*

MRS. EAMES. Evening, Wilbur. Coming to the party?

LARCH. Mrs. Eames!

MRS. EAMES. Have you met the Channing Peabodys? Let me introduce you ... *(Young Larch appears.)*

YOUNG LARCH. Hello, Wilbur.

LARCH. You.

YOUNG LARCH. You. *(Prostitute comes over to Young Larch.)*

PROSTITUTE. Evening, Doc. Care for an examination?

YOUNG LARCH. Ether. I think you forgot your ether.

LARCH. Ether.

ALL. Ether ...

MRS. EAMES. Please be discreet. Please be discreet. *(Mrs. Eames' Daughter grabs Young Larch.)*

MRS. EAMES' DAUGHTER. I ain't quick! What's it cost? I ain't quick!

ALL. Ether ...

MRS. EAMES. Rhymes with screams! *(Larch and Mrs. Eames dance. Young Larch and Mrs. Eames' Daughter dance.)* Ready, Wilbur?

LARCH. My God ...

MRS. EAMES. Ready?

ALL. Ready?

MRS. EAMES. Relax, Wilbur ... Relax ...

LARCH. Princes of Maine ... Kings of New England ...

ALL. Princes of Maine! Kings of New England!

LARCH. Princes of Maine! Kings of New England! *(They all dance off, swirling. Angel and Rose Rose rush on.)*

ANGEL. Rose!? Rose! Where're you going?

ROSE ROSE. Don't follow me, Angel. Let me be alone. *(A cramp doubles her over. She drops to her knees, as if she's been kicked. Angel catches her.)*

ANGEL. WHOA! You okay?

ROSE ROSE. I ... Yeah ...

ANGEL. You really hurt yourself on the bicycle, didn't you?

ROSE ROSE. I was tryin' to.

ANGEL. What?

ROSE ROSE. I was TRYIN' to hurt myself. But I don't think I hurt myself enough.

ANGEL. Enough for what?

ROSE ROSE. To lose the baby.

ANGEL. To lose the ... *(Pause.)* You. You're ... you're pregnant?

ROSE ROSE. Again. Again and again, I guess. Somebody must want me to keep havin' babies.

ANGEL. Who?

ROSE ROSE. Never mind.

ANGEL. Someone who's not here?

ROSE ROSE. Oh, he here. But never mind.

ANGEL. The father is here?

ROSE ROSE. The father of THIS one — yeah, he here.

ANGEL. Who is he?

ROSE ROSE. Never mind who he is.

ANGEL. Tell me!

ROSE ROSE. No!

ANGEL. Do you want the baby?

ROSE ROSE. I want the one I got. I don't want this other one! *(She strikes herself hard, then bends over in extreme pain. She lies down in the grass in a fetal position. Pause.)*

ANGEL. Rose?

ROSE ROSE. You wanna love me, or help me?

ANGEL. Both.

ROSE ROSE. Ain't no such thing as BOTH. If you smart, you just stick with helpin' me. That easier.

ANGEL. How? Anything.

ROSE ROSE. Just get me an abortion. I don't live 'round here, I don't know nobody to ask, and I got no money. Just get me an abortion ... *(Rose Rose exits as Homer, Candy, and Wally appear.)*

HOMER. She wouldn't tell you who the father is? *(Angel shakes his head.)*

WALLY. Oh, what's it matter, anyway ...

CANDY. The main thing is she doesn't want the baby. The main thing is to get her the abortion.

ANGEL. Only where? I won't have her go someplace dangerous. *(Pause.)*

WALLY. *(Quietly.)* Your dad can do it.

ANGEL. What?!

CANDY. Wally —

WALLY. Why shouldn't he know?

ANGEL. Know what? What are you talking about? Pop, you never told me ...

HOMER. *(Upset.)* There's a lot I haven't told you.

CANDY. Your father doesn't believe in it.

HOMER. I think it's wrong, but I think it should be everyone's personal choice!

ANGEL. That's fine! So this is HER choice!

HOMER. I'm sorry! I can't! I won't! You'll have to take her to St. Cloud's.

ANGEL. St. Cloud's?! But she doesn't want to have the baby. And she wouldn't want to leave it in the orphanage.

HOMER. She doesn't have to have the baby in St. Cloud's. She can have the abortion there. *(Pause.)*

CANDY. I had an abortion there once, Angel.

ANGEL. You did?

WALLY. At the time, we thought we'd always be able to have another baby.

CANDY. It was before Wally was hurt. It was before the war.

ANGEL. Doctor Larch does it?

HOMER. I'll call him right now. We'll put you and Rose Rose on the next train. *(Homer goes to the telephone. Angela appears, dazed. Nurse Edna appears from opposite.)*

NURSE EDNA. Angela. My God! What is it?

NURSE ANGELA. It's Doctor Larch ...

NURSE EDNA. Is he ...

NURSE ANGELA. Don't go in there.

NURSE EDNA. I want to see him. I HAVE TO — *(Nurse Angela holds Edna. The telephone rings.)*

HOMER. When Homer called St. Cloud's

NURSE CAROLINE. He got Nurse Caroline.

HOMER. Caroline? It's Homer. Let me speak with the old man.

NURSE CAROLINE. What do you want? Or have you changed

90

your mind?

HOMER. There's a friend of my son's. She's one of the migrants here. She's already got a baby who's got no father, and now she's going to have another.

NURSE CAROLINE. Then she'll have two.

HOMER. Caroline! Cut the shit. I want to talk to the old man.

NURSE CAROLINE. I'd like to talk to him, too. *(Pause.)* Larch is dead, Homer.

HOMER. Cut the shit.

NURSE CAROLINE. Too much ether.

HOMER. What? When ...

NURSE CAROLINE. Only a few hours ago.

HOMER. What...?

NURSE CAROLINE. There's no more Lord's work in St Cloud's. If you know someone who needs it, you'll have to do it yourself ... *(She hangs up.)*

HOMER. Let me talk to Edna ... Angela ... Hello? *(The nurses exit. Homer is alone onstage.)* She'd hung up on him. His ear rang. He heard the sound of the logs bashing together in the water that swept the Winkles away. His eyes had not stung so sharply since that night in the Drapers' furnace room, in Waterville, when he had dressed himself for his getaway. His throat had not ached so deeply — the pain pushing down, into his lungs — since that night he had cried himself to sleep while reading *Gray's Anatomy*, silently uttering the name of Fuzzy Stone. Homer shut his eyes. He watched *(The women appear.)*

WOMEN. The women getting off the train.

NURSE CAROLINE. They always looked a little lost.

OLIVE. And now they marched from the station.

CANDY. They marched uphill.

MRS. GROGAN. They were an army, advancing on the hospital orphanage,

ROSE ROSE. Bearing with them a single wound.

NURSE CAROLINE. Nurse Caroline was tough;

NURSE EDNA. But where would Nurse Edna

NURSE ANGELA. And Nurse Angela

NURSE ANGELA and NURSE EDNA. Go?

GROGAN. And what would happen to Mrs. Grogan?

91

MELONY. And Melony?

HOMER. If Melony were pregnant, I would help her. *(Pause.)* Whether I shall turn out to be the hero of my own life ... or whether that station will be held by anybody else ... these pages must show ... *(Pause.)*

ALL. Homer Wells

HOMER. Made up his mind.

CANDY, ROSE and MELONY. He would be a hero. *(Homer tentatively approaches Rose Rose. He brings her to a table set up for the abortion, Candy assisting him.)*

HOMER. This is a speculum. It may feel cold, but it doesn't hurt. You won't feel any of this.

ROSE ROSE. I never could do nothin' about it.

CANDY. Of course you couldn't.

ROSE ROSE. He hated the father of the first one. He cut him up. I know my father. He gonna want me back.

CANDY. He can't have you. You're going to be all right now. *(To Angel.)* Go stay with Wally, Angel.

ROSE ROSE. Yeah, you go away. *(Angel exits reluctantly.)*

HOMER. These are dilators.

ROSE ROSE. You done this before, ain't you?

CANDY. Homer knows what he's doing.

HOMER. I'm going to give you a light ether sedation. Just breathe normally.

ROSE ROSE. At the first whiff, she opened her eyes and turned her face away from the mask,

CANDY. But Candy put her hands at Rose Rose's temples and very gently moved her head into the right position.

HOMER. The first smell is the sharpest.

ROSE ROSE. Please. Have you done this before?

HOMER. I'm a good doctor. I really am. Just relax, and breathe normally.

CANDY. Don't be afraid,

ROSE ROSE. Rose Rose heard Candy tell her just before the ether began to take her out of her body. *(Pause.)* I can ride it.

HOMER. What?

ROSE ROSE. The bicycle. I can. Sand warm.

CANDY. The sand?

ROSE ROSE. The beach. Sand on my toes. Tide coming in. Water on my ankles. Nice. Nice. No big deal.

HOMER. Homer Wells, adjusting the speculum until he had a perfect view of the cervix, introduced the first dilator until the os opened like an eye looking back at him. The cervix looked softened and slightly enlarged, and it was bathed in a healthy, clear mucus — it was the most breathtaking pink color Homer had ever seen. *(Pause.)* He watched the cervix open until it opened wide enough. He chose the curette of the correct size. *(Pause.)* After the first one, this might get easier. If I can operate on Rose Rose, how can I refuse to help a stranger? How can I refuse anyone? Only a god makes that kind of decision. I'll just give them what they want. An orphan, or an abortion ... *(Rose Rose is wheeled off. Homer stands alone.)* Let us be happy for Doctor Larch. Doctor Larch has found a family. Good night, Doctor Larch ...

WOMEN. Good night, Doctor Larch. *(Homer exits. Angel enters.)*

ANGEL. In the morning, Angel noticed that Rose Rose and her daughter had gone. *(Homer appears, followed by Wally and Candy.)* I can't find her. I don't know where she is. Has anybody seen her? *(A shout. Jack comes running in.)*

JACK. Mistuh Wells! Mistuh Wells!

HOMER. Jack? What's going on?

JACK. You gotta come quickly! *(Homer and Angel exit. At the cider house, Mr. Rose sits outside in a Buddhist position, a blanket completely covering him except for his face. Muddy is with him. Wednesday comes out from the cider house.)*

MUDDY. You bring Mr. Rose some water, Wednesday?

WEDNESDAY. I got it right here. *(He puts water to Mr. Rose's lips. Mr. Rose drinks.)*

MR. ROSE. Where she get the knife, Muddy?

MUDDY. What knife?

MR. ROSE. It look like your knife — what I seen of it. *(Pause.)*

MUDDY. I gave it to her.

MR. ROSE. Thank you for doin' that, Muddy. If she gone with her thumb, I glad she got a knife with her. She good with that knife. She better with it than YOU ever be!

MUDDY. I know she good.

MR. ROSE. She almost the best. And who taught her?

MUDDY and WEDNESDAY. You did.

MR. ROSE. That right. That why she almost as good as me. *(Homer rushes in, followed by Angel and Hero.)* Who's that there?

HOMER. Mr. Rose. It's me. Homer. *(Homer comes in close to him.)*

MR. ROSE. *(Whispers.)* Hello, Homer. I didn't hurt her. I didn't touch her, Homer. I just love her, was all. You breakin' them rules, too, Homer. Say you know how I feel.

HOMER. I know how you feel.

MR. ROSE. *(Grinning.)* Right. *(Mr. Rose slowly rolls over on his side and tucks his knees up to his chest.)* I real tired of sittin' up. I gettin' sleepy. I didn't think it would take this long. It taken all day, but it felt like it was gonna go pretty fast.

HOMER. Let me look. I have to look.

MR. ROSE. Listen to me, Homer.

HOMER. You've been hemorrhaging all day ...

MR. ROSE. Listen. You tell them I stabbed myself. I meant to kill myself.

HOMER. There's no point, we can't even move him ...

MR. ROSE. I killed myself, otherwise why let myself bleed to death from a wound ...

HOMER. Shhh, quiet now ...

MR. ROSE. My daughter run away. And I so sorry that I stuck myself. You better say that what happen. Let me hear you say it!

MUDDY. That what happen.

WEDNESDAY. You kill yourself.

HERO. That what happen.

JACK. You stuck yourself.

MR. ROSE. You hearin' this right, Homer?

HOMER. Yes, Mr. Rose, I'm hearing it.

MR. ROSE. That how you report it ... According to the rules ...

HOMER. According to the rules ... *(Mr. Rose dies in Homer's arms. Migrants begin to sing "Amazing Grace" as they begin to carry Mr. Rose's body off. Muddy pulls Angel aside.)*

MUDDY. *(To Angel.)* She say to tell you you was the nicest. She say to tell your dad he a hero, and that you was the nicest.

ANGEL. She didn't say where she was going?

MUDDY. She don't know where she goin', Angel. She just know she gotta go.

94

ANGEL. But she could have stayed with us! W̲ɪ̲

MUDDY. I know she thought about it. You better t̲h̲.̲
too.

ANGEL. I love her!

MUDDY. Everybody love Rose Rose, that part of her problem.

ANGEL. This is different.

MUDDY. She know. She know who she is, too. But she also
know you don't know who you is, yet.

ANGEL. Muddy, if you should happen to see her —

MUDDY. I won't see her, Angel. She long gone. *(Angel goes to
Homer and cries on his shoulder.)*

HOMER. I know. I know ... *(Pause.)* How about going on a walk
with me? I've got a little story for you. *(Homer and Angel go up and
sit on the roof. Candy appears with Wally.)*

CANDY. Candy, who drove by the cider house and saw them sitting up on the roof, was worried about how cold they must be. But
she didn't interrupt them. She just kept driving. She hoped the
truth would keep them warm. *(She wheels Wally.)*

WALLY. Where are we going?

CANDY. My father's dock.

WALLY. But that dock's been blown oversea long ago.

CANDY. We'll go as near to it as we can get. *(They drive.)* She
drove near to the old pilings of what had been her father's dock —
where she and Wally had spent so many evenings, so long ago. *(She
carries Wally, out of the wheelchair, and sets him down, holding him.)*

WALLY. Look at that coastline.

CANDY. Yes. Look.

WALLY. And out there must be Europe.

CANDY. Yes.

WALLY. This is fun. *(She hugs him tightly around his arms and his
chest, and squeezes his withered hips with her legs.)*

CANDY. I love you, Wally.

WALLY. Good.

CANDY. And I want to tell you a story ... *(Sound of train whistle.
Homer, Wally and Candy exit.)*

STATIONMASTER. Now arriving, St. Cloud's. Step off for St.
Cloud's! St. Cloud's, Maine! *(Homer appears, dressed as a doctor,
carrying the doctor's bag.)*

95

ANGEL. St. Cloud's?

HOMER. The orphanage. I used to be an orphan here. Now I'm the new doctor.

STATIONMASTER. Oh! I thought you looked familiar! *(He bows and shakes Homer's hand.)* We'll send your bags up. *(A thin young woman wearing a muskrat coat with a scarf and ski hat has also gotten off the train, and hung back on the platform. Homer starts to walk up the hill.)*

THIN WOMAN. Is this the way to the orphanage?

HOMER. Right.

THIN WOMAN. Are you the doctor?

HOMER. Yes. I'm Doctor Stone. *(He takes her arm.)* May I help you? *(The bell rings. Nurse Angela appears, throwing her arms around Homer's neck.)*

NURSE ANGELA. Oh, Homer! I knew you'd be back!

HOMER. *(Whispers.)* Call me Fuzzy. *(As they embrace, the orphans, Nurse Caroline, Nurse Edna and Mrs. Grogan all appear. Homer reads to the orphans.)* Great Expectations, Chapter Fifty-Four … "It was one of those March days when the sun shines hot and the wind blows cold — *(Homer continues reading as Candy and Wally appear.)* — when it is summer in the light, and winter in the shade. We had our pea-coats with us, and I took a bag. Where I might go, what I might do, or when I might return were questions utterly unknown to me, nor did I vex my mind with them … "

CANDY. In the years to come, Candy and Wally Worthington would throw themselves full tilt into apple farming.

WALLY. Wally would serve two terms as president of the Maine Horticultural Society.

CANDY. Candy would serve a term as director of the New York – New England Apple Institute. *(Angel appears.)*

ANGEL. And Angel Wells, whom Rose Rose had introduced to love and to imagination, would one day be a novelist.

WALLY. The kid's got fiction in his blood.

HOMER. When he was tired or plagued with insomnia, or both, Homer would miss Angel, or he would think of Candy. Sometimes he longed to carry Wally into the surf, or to fly with him. But, at least he knew —

ANGEL, CANDY, WALLY and HOMER. They would all spend

96

Christmas and the holidays together.

CANDY. After a while, Homer would write to Candy and say that he had become a socialist,

HOMER. Or, at least, that he'd become sympathetic to socialist views.

CANDY. Candy understood by this confession that Homer was sleeping with Nurse Caroline

NURSE CAROLINE. Which she also understood would be good for them —

HOMER. That is, it was good for Homer

NURSE CAROLINE. And for Nurse Caroline,

CANDY. And it was good for Candy, too.

NURSE EDNA. For a while, Doctor Stone lacked only one thing —

NURSE ANGELA. And he was about to order it when one came unordered to him.

MRS. GROGAN. As if from God. *(Stationmaster appears.)*

STATIONMASTER. Doctor Stone, there's a body come in for you down at the railroad station. It's addressed to you. From the hospital in Bath.

HOMER. Must be some mistake. *(The body is brought in. Homer stares at it.)*

STATIONMASTER. Doctor Stone? You okay?

HOMER. Please. Let me be alone with her. *(The Stationmaster nods and retreats. Lorna appears.)*

LORNA. She had requested this use of her body. She had seen a photograph in the Bath paper, together with an article revealing Doctor Stone's appointment in St. Cloud's. In the event of her death, which was caused by an electrical accident, she had instructed me to send her body to Doctor Stone in St. Cloud's. She said she might be of some use to him, finally. *(Homer holds Melony's body.)*

LORNA. She was a daydreamer, Homer.

HOMER. All orphans are daydreamers.

LORNA. You was her hero, finally. *(Stationmaster returns.)*

STATIONMASTER. Should I send it back, Doctor?

HOMER. No. She belongs here. She belongs up the hill.

STATIONMASTER. You going to use her, then?

HOMER. Use her? No. She ... she has been used enough. *(As Melony is taken up the hill, Mrs. Grogan follows.)*

MRS. GROGAN. Oh Lord, support us all the day long — *(Mrs. Grogan continues the prayer as the group begins to disperse and Homer speaks.)* — until the shadows lengthen and the evening comes, and the busy world is hushed, and the fever of life is over, and our work is done. Then in thy mercy grant us a safe lodging, and a holy rest ...

HOMER. Oh, Melony. I always expected a lot from you. But you gave me more than I ever dreamed. You ... you truly educated me. You showed me the light. You ... you were more Sunshine than I ever was.

MRS. GROGAN. *(Finishing the prayer.)* ... and peace at the last. *(Pause.)*

HOMER. Let us be happy for Melony. Melony has found a family. *(The group disperses.)*

ALL. Amen. *(Nurse Caroline sees a huge book Homer is holding.)*

NURSE CAROLINE. What are you reading?

HOMER. This, Larch's journal. It is my new education, Caroline.

NURSE CAROLINE. *(Reads.)* "A Brief History of St. Cloud's" ...

HOMER. In this pursuit, Homer would have

NURSE ANGELA. Nurse Angela's

NURSE EDNA. and Nurse Edna's

MRS. GROGAN. and Mrs. Grogan's

NURSE CAROLINE. and Nurse Caroline's tireless company.

NURSE CAROLINE, NURSE EDNA and NURSE ANGELA. For by this pursuit they would keep Wilbur Larch alive.

HOMER. And as he grew older, Homer Wells would take special comfort in an unexplained revelation he found in the writings of Wilbur Larch. *(Larch appears.)*

LARCH. Tell Doctor Stone —

HOMER. And this was his very last entry; these were Wilbur Larch's last words:

LARCH. Tell Doctor Stone there is absolutely nothing wrong with Homer's heart. *(The company has fully gathered now. They sing.)*

HOMER. To Nurse Edna,

NURSE EDNA. Who was in love,

HOMER. And to Nurse Angela,

NURSE ANGELA. Who wasn't,

HOMER. But who had in her wisdom named both Homer Wells and Fuzzy Stone,

NURSE ANGELA. There was no fault to be found in the hearts of either Doctor Stone or Doctor Larch,

NURSE EDNA. Who were, if there ever were,

ENTIRE COMPANY. Princes of Maine, Kings of New England!

HOMER and LARCH. Good night! *(Homer and Larch together. The company gathered around them.)*

The End.

PROPERTY LIST

Paper and writing utensil
Letters
Surgical masks
Books
Trees
Car keys (WALLY)
Can of insecticide spray (WALLY)
Condom (HERB)
Mail (LARCH, NURSE ANGELA, HOMER)
Typewriter (NURSE EDNA/NURSE ANGELA)
Cup of cider (MR. ROSE)
Pieces of paper (LARCH)
Ball bearing (LORNA)
Clump of hair (CANDY)
Beers (MELONY, LORNA)
Flying uniform (WALLY)
Mitten full of ball bearings (LORNA), p. 38
Pamphlets (MRS. GROGAN)
Cup of tea (OLIVE)
Drink (LARCH)
Spade (HOMER)
Baby (LARCH, HOMER, CANDY)
Telegram (OLIVE, CANDY)
Box containing an Army surplus coat with money, copper wire, and wire-cutters in pockets (MELONY)
Black bag (LARCH, HOMER)
Wrapping materials (LARCH)
Framed newspaper article (MELONY)
Bucket (ROSE ROSE)
Something to cover herself with (ROSE ROSE)
Hat/cap (ANGEL)
Apple (CANDY)
Candle (CANDY, MR. ROSE)
Pizza (MELONY)
Sweatshirt (ROSE ROSE)
Ether apparatus (LARCH)

Phone (HOMER, NURSE CAROLINE)
Blanket (MR. ROSE)
Cup of water (WEDNESDAY)
Journal (HOMER)

SOUND EFFECTS

Barking dogs
Movie sounds and music
Factory whistle
River
Radio broadcast
Bomber plane
Bomber planes, bombing, and sirens
Explosion
Bell
Train whistle
Car horn
Jukebox
Music
Telephone

NEW PLAYS

★ **HONOUR by Joanna Murray-Smith.** In a series of intense confrontations, a wife, husband, lover and daughter negotiate the forces of passion, history, responsibility and honour. "HONOUR makes for surprisingly interesting viewing. Tight, crackling dialogue (usually played out in punchy verbal duels) captures characters unable to deal with emotions ... Murray-Smith effectively places her characters in situations that strip away pretense." –*Variety* "... the play's virtues are strong: a distinctive theatrical voice, passionate concerns ... HONOUR might just capture a few honors of its own." –*Time Out Magazine* [1M, 3W] ISBN: 0-8222-1683-3

★ **MR. PETERS' CONNECTIONS by Arthur Miller.** Mr. Miller describes the protagonist as existing in a dream-like state when the mind is "freed to roam from real memories to conjectures, from trivialities to tragic insights, from terror of death to glorying in one's being alive." With this memory play, the Tony Award and Pulitzer Prize-winner reaffirms his stature as the world's foremost dramatist. "... a cross between Joycean stream-of-consciousness and Strindberg's dream plays, sweetened with a dose of William Saroyan's philosophical whimsy ... CONNECTIONS is most intriguing ..." –*The NY Times* [5M, 3W] ISBN: 0-8222-1687-6

★ **THE WAITING ROOM by Lisa Loomer.** Three women from different centuries meet in a doctor's waiting room in this dark comedy about the timeless quest for beauty – and its cost. "... THE WAITING ROOM ... is a bold, risky melange of conflicting elements that is ... terrifically moving ... There's no resisting the fierce emotional pull of the play." –*The NY Times* "... one of the high points of this year's Off-Broadway season ... THE WAITING ROOM is well worth a visit." –*Back Stage* [7M, 4W, flexible casting] ISBN: 0-8222-1594-2

★ **THE OLD SETTLER by John Henry Redwood.** A sweet-natured comedy about two church-going sisters in 1943 Harlem and the handsome young man who rents a room in their apartment. "For all of its decent sentiments, THE OLD SETTLER avoids sentimentality. It has the authenticity and lack of pretense of an Early American sampler." –*The NY Times* "We've had some fine plays Off-Broadway this season, and this is one of the best." –*The NY Post* [1M, 3W] ISBN: 0-8-222-1642-6

★ **LAST TRAIN TO NIBROC by Arlene Hutton.** In 1940 two young strangers share a seat on a train bound east only to find their paths will cross again. "All aboard. LAST TRAIN TO NIBROC is a sweetly told little chamber romance." –*Show Business* "... [a] gently charming little play, reminiscent of Thornton Wilder in its look at rustic Americans who are to be treasured for their simplicity and directness ..." –*Associated Press* "The old formula of boy wins girls, boy loses girl, boy wins girl still works ... [a] well-made play that perfectly captures a slice of small-town-life-gone-by." –*Back Stage* [1M, 1W] ISBN: 0-8222-1753-8

★ **OVER THE RIVER AND THROUGH THE WOODS by Joe DiPietro.** Nick sees both sets of his grandparents every Sunday for dinner. This is routine until he has to tell them that he's been offered a dream job in Seattle. The news doesn't sit so well. "A hilarious family comedy that is even funnier than his long running musical revue *I Love You, You're Perfect, Now Change.*" –*Back Stage* "Loaded with laughs every step of the way." –*Star-Ledger* [3M, 3W] ISBN: 0-8222-1712-0

★ **SIDE MAN by Warren Leight.** 1999 Tony Award winner. This is the story of a broken family and the decline of jazz as popular entertainment. "... a tender, deeply personal memory play about the turmoil in the family of a jazz musician as his career crumbles at the dawn of the age of rock-and-roll ..." –*The NY Times* "[SIDE MAN] is an elegy for two things – a lost world and a lost love. When the two notes sound together in harmony, it is moving and graceful ..." –*The NY Daily News* "An atmospheric memory play ... with crisp dialogue and clearly drawn characters ... reflects the passing of an era with persuasive insight ... The joy and despair of the musicians is skillfully illustrated." –*Variety* [5M, 3W] ISBN: 0-8222-1721-X

DRAMATISTS PLAY SERVICE, INC.
440 Park Avenue South, New York, NY 10016 212-683-8960 Fax 212-213-1539
postmaster@dramatists.com www.dramatists.com

NEW PLAYS

★ **CLOSER by Patrick Marber.** Winner of the 1998 Olivier Award for Best Play and the 1999 New York Drama Critics Circle Award for Best Foreign Play. Four lives intertwine over the course of four and a half years in this densely plotted, stinging look at modern love and betrayal. "CLOSER is a sad, savvy, often funny play that casts a steely, unblinking gaze at the world of relationships and lets you come to your own conclusions ... CLOSER does not merely hold your attention; it burrows into you." –*New York Magazine* "A powerful, darkly funny play about the cosmic collision between the sun of love and the comet of desire." –*Newsweek Magazine* [2M, 2W] ISBN: 0-8222-1722-8

★ **THE MOST FABULOUS STORY EVER TOLD by Paul Rudnick.** A stage manager, headset and prompt book at hand, brings the house lights to half, then dark, and cues the creation of the world. Throughout the play, she's in control of everything. In other words, she's either God, or she thinks she is. "Line by line, Mr. Rudnick may be the funniest writer for the stage in the United States today ... One-liners, epigrams, withering put-downs and flashing repartee: These are the candles that Mr. Rudnick lights instead of cursing the darkness ... a testament to the virtues of laughing ... and in laughter, there is something like the memory of Eden." –*The NY Times* "Funny it is ... consistently, rapaciously, deliriously ... easily the funniest play in town." –*Variety* [4M, 5W] ISBN: 0-8222-1720-1

★ **A DOLL'S HOUSE by Henrik Ibsen, adapted by Frank McGuinness.** Winner of the 1997 Tony Award for Best Revival. "New, raw, gut-twisting and gripping. Easily the hottest drama this season." –*USA Today* "Bold, brilliant and alive." –*The Wall Street Journal* "A thunderclap of an evening that takes your breath away." –*Time Magazine* [4M, 4W, 2 boys] ISBN: 0-8222-1636-1

★ **THE HERBAL BED by Peter Whelan.** The play is based on actual events which occurred in Stratford-upon-Avon in the summer of 1613, when William Shakespeare's elder daughter was publicly accused of having a sexual liaison with a married neighbor and family friend. "In his probing new play, THE HERBAL BED ... Peter Whelan muses about a sidelong event in the life of Shakespeare's family and creates a finely textured tapestry of love and lies in the early 17th-century Stratford." –*The NY Times* "It is a first rate drama with interesting moral issues of truth and expediency." –*The NY Post* [5M, 3W] ISBN: 0-8222-1675-2

★ **SNAKEBIT by David Marshall Grant.** A study of modern friendship when put to the test. "... a rather smart and absorbing evening of water-cooler theater, the intimate sort of Off-Broadway experience that has you picking apart the recognizable characters long after the curtain calls." –*The NY Times* "Off-Broadway keeps on presenting us with compelling reasons for going to the theater. The latest is SNAKEBIT, David Marshall Grant's smart new comic drama about being thirtysomething and losing one's way in life." –*The NY Daily News* [3M, 1W] ISBN: 0-8222-1724-4

★ **A QUESTION OF MERCY by David Rabe.** The Obie Award-winning playwright probes the sensitive and controversial issue of doctor-assisted suicide in the age of AIDS in this poignant drama. "There are many devastating ironies in Mr. Rabe's beautifully considered, piercingly clear-eyed work ..." –*The NY Times* "With unsettling candor and disturbing insight, the play arouses pity and understanding of a troubling subject ... Rabe's provocative tale is an affirmation of dignity that rings clear and true." –*Variety* [6M, 1W] ISBN: 0-8222-1643-4

★ **DIMLY PERCEIVED THREATS TO THE SYSTEM by Jon Klein.** Reality and fantasy overlap with hilarious results as this unforgettable family attempts to survive the nineties. "Here's a play whose point about fractured families goes to the heart, mind – and ears." –*The Washington Post* "... an end-of-the millennium comedy about a family on the verge of a nervous breakdown ... Trenchant and hilarious ..." –*The Baltimore Sun* [2M, 4W] ISBN: 0-8222-1677-9

DRAMATISTS PLAY SERVICE, INC.
440 Park Avenue South, New York, NY 10016 212-683-8960 Fax 212-213-1539
postmaster@dramatists.com www.dramatists.com